"Beyond sharing his successful restaurant dishes a̶
occasional cocktail, Anthony Rose serves up instr̶
party fare and for foods to take camping or to th̶
does an extended riff on 'le hamburger.' All this̶
bad-boy, joking style that tells us to let go and have fun,
rather than worrying about the details."

Naomi Duguid,

award-winning author of Burma and Taste of Persia

"The Last Schmaltz showcases Tony's love for food, people, and life.
The warm, casual style portrayed in all his restaurants creates the
ultimate cross-cultural comfort food recipes with intense flavor.
Whether you start with the slow roasted cauliflower with halloumi,
tahini and pomegranate seeds; a cheesy patty melt; or Fat Pasha
hummus, you will soon have a dog-eared copy of this book as you
can't help but make every recipe. And if anyone can bring back
herring, Tony will with his passion and pulpit for great food."

Emily Luchetti,

chief pastry officer and co-author of The Fearless Baker

Whether you know him as Toronto's King of Comfort Food,
the Don of Dupont, or the Sultan of Smoked Meat, a conversation
about the food and restaurant scene in Toronto isn't complete
without mention of Anthony Rose. From his famous Fat Pasha
Cauliflower (which may or may not have caused the Great Cauliflower
Shortage of 2016) and Rose and Sons Patty Melt to his Pork Belly
Fried Rice and Nutella Babka Bread Pudding, Anthony's dishes have
consistently made waves in the culinary community. Now, in his
first cookbook, he has teamed up with internationally-renowned
food and travel writer Chris Johns to share his most famous
recipes and stories.

Be amazed by the reactions Anthony received when he ingeniously
invented a dish called the "All-Day Breakfast." Thrill at the
wonder Anthony felt when, as a young Jewish kid, he tasted the
illicit lusciousness of bacon for the first time. Or discover
the secret ingredient to the perfect shore lunch on a camping
trip (hint: it's foie gras).

Often funny, sometimes ridiculous, but always delicious,
The Last Schmaltz is a peek into the mind of a much-loved
chef at the top of his culinary game.

SCHMALTZ (Yiddish):
1. melted chicken fat.
2. Excessive sentimentality;
   overly emotional and
   sentimental behavior.

ANTHONY *Rose*
and
CHRIS *Johns*

A VERY SERIOUS COOKBOOK

MALTZ

appetite
by RANDOM HOUSE

Appetite by Random House ® and colophon are
registered trademarks of Penguin Random House LLC.

Library and Archives of Canada Cataloguing in
Publication is available upon request.

ISBN: 978-0-14-753003-5
eBook ISBN: 978-0-14-753004-2

Cover and book design by
CS Richardson & Andrew Roberts
Photography by Kayla Rocca
Cover image: (chicken) © Morphart Creation /
Shutterstock.com
Interior backgrounds © wanchai and Prostock-
studio, both Shutterstock.com

Excerpt from "Ode to an Artichoke" translated by
Stephen Mitchell from *The Poetry of Pablo Neruda*
by Pablo Neruda, edited by Ilan Stavans.
Copyright © 2003 by Pablo Neruda and Fundación
Pablo Neruda. Reprinted by permission of
Farrar, Straus and Giroux.

Excerpt from "Oda a la alcachofa",
Odas Elementales © 1954, Fundación Pablo Neruda

Printed and bound in China

Published in Canada by Appetite by Random House ®,
a division of Penguin Random House LLC.

www.penguinrandomhouse.ca

10 9 8 7 6 5 4 3 2 1

appetite
by RANDOM HOUSE | Penguin
Random House
Canada

For Simon Thorne Rose,
my favorite son.
You make it all worthwhile.
I love you so much.

And for Robert Wilder,
my third wife.
Thanks for the chocolate idea we never did.
Sorry I didn't eat with you.
So much more to come.

-ANTHONY ROSE

For Jillian and Harper Grace, as always.

-CHRIS JOHNS

IG ROW

EST.2013

OW START

NEW & SOUR PICKLE APPETIZER ..11

Mozzarella &Roast Garlic Bread ..13

ESAR SALAD ..14
ED Croutons, Parmesan Dressing, Anchovies
BBQ Crow Bacon ..+ 5

HEAD TROUT POKE ..16
CHILI, GINGER, SOY, FURIKAKE, CHIPS

ED SHRIMP DIABLO ..18
hili Hot Sauce, Guacamole, Pepitas

HOT SMOKED REUB

BRISKET MOZZARELLA SAUERKRAUT

★★★★★★ $24 ★★★

WEEKEN
CARVERY
fridays & saturdays until sold out

SMOKED PRIME RIB OF B
HORSERADISH & MUSTARD CREAM ★ GRAVY ★ SIMPLE GOOD MA

MOKED OR GRILL

TONGUE ..13
radish & beetroot salsa

TH PORK BELLY ..15
hili peppers & creamed onions

ISED BEEF CHEEK
A LA BOURGIGNON ..24
ooms, carrots, pearl onions

Y BACK RIBS FULL SLAB ..32
HALF SLAB ..17
noked ancho & molasses BBQ sauce

Jw Bir
sour pickle brined, salsa

CROW CURED PEAMEAL BACC
hard apple cider & cranberry

Rainbow Trou
JERK SAUCE & EZELL'S SWEET

1LB FLANK STEA
grilled broccoli. sage & walnu

ONE WHOLE FIS
winter cranberry bean suc

T CROW

RK&BEANS
CHUP CHIPS 7
ato GRATIN
ello MUSHROOMS

SWEET Cr

OAT & APPLE

BAKERMANS
FUDGE BROWNIE

TABLE SIDE

$9 EVOO

FATTOUSH $16
CHOPPED ISRAELI SALAD W/ ZA'TAAR PITA CHIPS

$3
$2

CHOPPED LIVER SAMMIES ROUMANIAN $16
SCHMALTZ, GRIBENES, ONIONS, RADISH, EGG, GRATEFUL BREAD CHALLAH

FALAFEL $9
TAHINI, LEMON, ONIONS

LABNEH $5
EVOO, ZATAAR

PICKLES $9
NEW, SOUR, HOT, OLIVES

O O O O O O O O O O O O O O

FAT PASHA

ICY

SUCCU

DRY AGED ← → GRILLED

RIBEYE STEAK
WITH ZA'TAAR BUTTER

GREEN TAHINI & BLACK OLIVE RELISH

WITH

LAMB CHOPS

O O O O O O O O O O O O O

VEGETABLES

ROAST CAULIFLOWER HEAD 1/2 $12
TAHINI, PINENUT, POMEGRANATE & HALLOUMI FULL $18

YUKON GOLD FF
SMOKED PAPRIKA MAYO $7

$10

CHILI & GARLIC VEGETABLE KEBAB AMBA

GRILLED ESCAROLE $12

SHOW SOME LOVE TO THE CHEFS $16

Sweet Fern and Bear Lard

A Story of People Places & Things like Food, Resturants, Art and M.C.

By

Anthony Rose and Chris Schiss
4 Blessings & Om Shanti's
NOT a Lifestyle Book

Foreword by Rachel Mcadams w/
Margaret Atwood

Château Anthony Rose

Bar Mitzvah Vintage
16 November 1985
MIS EN BOUTEILLE AU CHATEAU

SCUMBAGS AND SUPERSTARS

"What's next and Who Cares"

"This is the Most important Work of Non-Fiction Fiction
I have ever Read. All schools should have this Tome as
Mandatory Reading". Ottolenghi

Cover By
Ed

Foreword by
John Irving

CONTENTS

Sometimes I look at Anthony and I think to myself, "oh my god—where did you come from?!" I find myself wondering where he got his sense of humor and edginess. And while I wasn't surprised to learn that he was writing a cookbook, it gave me pause to remember my shy, introverted little boy who was more interested in taking apart his toys than being creative.

Although I cooked often when my three kids were young, it always took place late at night, after they had gone to bed. I looked at it as my quiet time. And Anthony didn't show much interest in either cooking or adventurous eating. His favorite food was a burger, but he only wanted to eat the hamburger bun and as much ketchup as possible. My husband, Joel, and I would look at each other in dismay, wishing for some decorum at the table. Anthony never joined me in the kitchen, but I would hear after-the-fact that when Joel and I were away, Anthony would assume the role of head chef and prepare meals for his brother and sister.

When Anthony told us that he wanted to attend culinary school instead of finishing university, I knew it would be good for him to get away from the pressures at home and figure out who he really wanted to be. But I had no idea that culinary school would introduce him to his passion and become such an important part of his life's trajectory.

Of course, that's exactly what happened. He worked hard and grew into himself. He figured out what made him happy, and became a highly-respected chef—if you ask me, his pastrami is the best you'll have anywhere, ever. His Fat Pasha chicken is fantastic. His spreads and dips are wonderful. He does a dynamite chicken soup (it started as my recipe, but who's keeping track?). And don't even get me started on his hamburgers and patty melts.

This book, The Last Schmaltz, is another step in that remarkable trajectory. Together with Chris, Anthony has put together something genuinely impressive. It is not only the recipes and stories of a confident, knowledgeable chef, but a true expression of my fabulous son. I am so proud to introduce Anthony to readers everywhere, and while I'm still not sure where his personality came from, I love everything about him.

                                        —LINDA ROSE, a.k.a. Anthony's Mom

Anthony Rose and Chris Johns. Name a more iconic duo. I'll wait.

We'll accept Starsky and Hutch, Hall and Oates, a platonic Bert and Ernie, or those two weird old dudes down at the end of the street who are always standing around, watching the construction. Everyone else, step aside.

In the movie version of this book, Anthony and I will meet cute: both reaching for the last breaded imitation scallop at the all-you-can-eat buffet, or bumping peanut butter and banana cones at a crowded ice-cream parlor. We might meet while building a little log cabin out of waffles at a diner before discovering that one of us has short-term memory loss and learning that the other person must be won over anew each day. Okay, that last one's the plot of the 2004 Adam Sandler, Drew Barrymore classic, 50 First Dates, but you get the picture.

In reality, our relationship started out a little more pragmatically.

Anthony was already working on this book before I was brought in. And I was already working on another book (A Taste of Prince Edward County) before I met with Anthony. Coincidentally, a few weeks before this momentous partnership took shape, my agent, who lives almost exactly midway between Rose and Sons/Big Crow and Bar Begonia/Madame Boeuf, contacted Anthony to see if he was ready to write a book and if he wanted to work together. Anthony responded with something like "Thanks, but no thanks. I'm already writing a book." At some point, though, he realized that his process of "writing a book" was turning out to be something more akin to an extended therapy session with his amanuensis.

"When I first met you, I was maybe six months in and hadn't done very much," Anthony admits. "I'd never written a book before, and the whole thing was so confusing, I couldn't wrap my mind around it. I was busy and I'm a daydreamer, and I finally figured out—months after my editor gently told me the same thing—that I was getting nowhere fast."

That's probably when our mutual editor, the inimitable Zoe Maslow, came up with what will surely be remembered as her greatest idea of all time and suggested that Anthony and I work together.

I don't think we'd actually met in person at that point. I'd interviewed him once or twice for stories I was writing over the years when he was at the Drake or when he'd just opened Rose and Sons, but we'd never had a face-to-face. I followed his career, though, and remembered he'd always been fun to interview. He gave good quotes and was the kind of person who could speak in complete sentences, so I figured he was someone I could work with. More importantly, I'd eaten at most of the restaurants and knew they were legit.

We arranged to meet at the incredibly impressive swinging bachelor pad, all whitewashed walls and good leather furniture, that Anthony kept as an office above Swan. Right away, we both knew we didn't want to make a basic dump-and-stir cookbook or a gimmicky mass-market paperback: 2-Minute Weekday Lifesavers, Dumpster Diving for Dummies, and The Wiccan Vegan were all ruled out, so we decided on this format. The Last Schmaltz is built around recipes from Anthony's seven restaurants, with a bonus chapter on the various extracurricular adventures we had during the year and a half that we worked on the book.

By throwing a big party at each of the restaurants and using it as a jumping-off point to talk about the history of the place, where it fits in Anthony's empire, and what it represents, we are paying homage to Anthony's favorite book of all time: Jeremiah Tower's New American Classics. "That book's been my go-to for 25 years," Anthony says. "His book is amazing, because it's ridiculous. There are his stories about his great Russian uncle eating a blini and the butter running down his hand. There are his pictures, too: all these beautiful boys in hunting gear in the misty valley in Napa with shotguns and a blanket, just eating a picnic. It's so over the top, it's amazing."

As for the recipes, some are drawn from the parties and some are favorites from the restaurants. As you read through each chapter, you'll probably notice how so many of the restaurants started out as these amorphous ideas and slowly evolved into what they are today. That's sort of how this book came together too. With each celebration, the concept of the book came more and more into focus until finally, just as we were finishing the last draft of the manuscript, we came up with a title.

For months, we'd been trying to persuade our editor to let us call the book Sweet Fern and Bear Lard in honor of an ancient Ojibwe recipe for mosquito repellent that we learned about while on a canoe trip in Temagami (see chapter 8), but she and the publisher weren't having it. Hundreds of ideas, many of them shockingly inappropriate, were floated and rejected before we finally hit upon the current title. Although it won't prevent mosquito bites, we still love it because it references one of the greatest concert films ever made (featuring a Canadian band, thank you very much) and celebrates rendered chicken fat. As to how serious this book is, we'll leave that up to you to decide.

We had a great time putting The Last Schmaltz together and hope you'll have just as much fun reading about it and cooking from it. Dig in!

and the gentle
artichoke
stood there in the garden,
dressed as a warrior,
burnished
like a pomegranate,
proud,
and one day
along with the others
in large willow baskets, it traveled
to the market to realize its dream:
the army.

from ODE TO AN ARTICHOKE
by Pablo Neruda

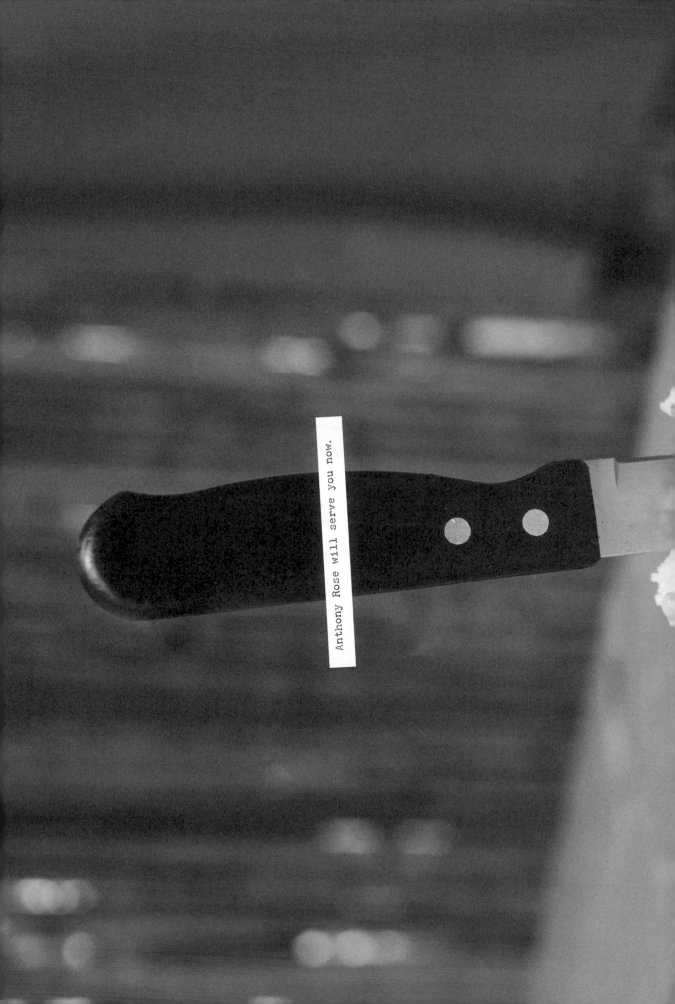

Anthony Rose will serve you now.

ROSE AND SONS

IT'S LADIES' NIGHT AND KOOL & THE GANG'S BEEN RUNNING THROUGH my
head all day. Anthony's hosting a ladies' night at Rose and Sons tonight and,
despite the significant handicap of not being a lady, I'm invited. The earworm
is my mind's way of dealing with the pressure.

Rose and Sons—the eclectic little rock and roll diner with the vintage cookbooks on the shelves, First Growth wine crates on the walls, and party fries
on the menu—was Anthony's first restaurant.

By 2012, he'd decided to leave his position as executive chef at the Drake
Hotel, where he'd earned an outsized reputation cooking outsized food, in
order to open his own place. That same year, he met the tech executive Robert
Wilder, who would become his business partner/friend/guru.

One day, Anthony's brother saw a sign in the window of a local diner, People's
Foods, saying it was closing. People's Foods was an institution. It had been
around for nearly 50 years. Everyone went there for grilled cheese on Wonder
Bread, chicken souvlaki plates, and club sandwiches.

Anthony knew this was the place.

"When we first walked in here, everything was in disrepair," Anthony says.
"The whole place was fucking gross. And we knew we wanted it right away."

Anthony and Robert got in and immediately started throwing things out. They
jackhammered the floor to take the old tile up, but kept most of the kitchen
as it was other than cleaning it and putting new motors in all the appliances.

"As a chef, opening your first place is very personal," Anthony says.
"Everything you make, you're putting it out there for someone to judge.
To love or to hate. You're just trying to make food that someone will love.
Essentially, you're inviting people into your heart."

Anthony was never going to do fine dining. "I love a diner," he says. "I do
that." And "diner" was exactly what People's called out for. It quickly became
clear that the menu would include items like an all-day breakfast, a patty
melt—still one of the best burgers in the city—and fried chicken. "From the
beginning, it was deep, dark, glorified stoner food," Anthony says.

Unlike most diners, People's included, Rose and Sons also built a great wine
list—small but carefully edited—and one of the city's best bourbon collections.
In fact, it was Anthony's love of bourbon that helped inspire the theme for
tonight's ladies' night: steak and whisky.

Dave Mitton—burly, bearded, always looks like he's ready to go panning for
gold at a moment's notice—is also the global ambassador for Lot No. 40 and
Pike Creek. And he's the cohost for tonight's party. He's at the front door of
the diner greeting everyone when I roll up. Soon he'll start pouring out
selections from his portfolio and giving everyone a bit of an education on
what makes Canadian whisky unique and special. To accompany all the booze,
Anthony and chef de cuisine Jesse Grasso have put together a menu that pays
homage to the great steak houses of the world.

The ladies, both regulars and first-timers, a couple celebrating birthdays, arrive in a quiet, orderly manner.

"This is our second annual ladies' night," Anthony announces when all the ladies (and me) are comfortably settled in their booths. "The first one was at Fat Pasha, which was incredible. It was hard to find a better idea than that, so we got Dave instead."

One of the ladies bangs out a rim shot with her cutlery and water glass. Later, I'll identify this as the moment when things began to unravel.

Before food there is whisky. Dave pours out shots of the Pike Creek 10-year-old barrel-aged and the Lot 40 rye. The conversation grows louder.

"At any point during the night, if you want any more booze, just ask for more booze," Anthony announces. "Also, do not drink and drive."

Dinner starts to arrive and, with it, still more whisky. There's Gooderham & Worts Four Grain along with the shrimp cocktail. Plump little suckers hang off the edge of a big coupe glass over a mound of shaved ice. A few sprigs of chervil are scattered across the top, and a tiny bowl filled with zippy cocktail sauce lies smack-dab in the middle.

This old-school, so-square-it's-hip dish captures Anthony's cooking in a nutshell—well, a shrimp shell. It's a bit kitschy, but undeniably delicious. Most shrimp rings go wrong by being half-frozen boxes of zombie crustaceans dragged out of the dusty confines of a discount grocer's freezer table; Anthony's version is built around chubby, fresh shrimp, expertly presented and buoyed by the zesty kick of a superb cocktail sauce. It's a reminder of why everyone loved this dish in the first place and why, when done properly, it's a classic.

Somehow, over the ever-increasing din, Dave manages to get people's attention long enough to explain the difference between "whiskey" and "whisky." "If your country doesn't have an 'e' in it, there's no 'e' in whisky," he says. "Take off your shirt," someone heckles in response. Dave demurs.

The kitchen, possibly in an effort to mollify the ladies, sends out more food. There's whipped garlic butter for spreading on steamy focaccia the texture of angel food cake, and little brown pots of mustard to go with thick slices of roast beef. One of the guests calls for the beef bones and soon all decorum is abandoned as a few barbarians, myself included, start gnawing away. Marrow gets everywhere.

By the time dessert arrives—New York-style cheesecake with wild blueberry compote and chantilly cream—the dancing has started. The whisky is flowing freely now and the laughter has taken on a slightly feral edge. I get involved in some kind of selfie situation. At some point, Anthony, behind the bar, is shirtless. Kool & the Gang never does come on the stereo, but as I get up to bust a move, it seems the ladies have, at last, accepted me into their night.

Anyone interested in throwing caution to the wind and recreating the second annual ladies' night meal will find some of the recipes in this chapter, along with a selection of other favorite "glorified stoner" dishes from the Rose and Sons canon.

[ROSE AND SONS]

Canadian Whiskey vs American

SUBLIME

MADE

Montreal Stoner
cheating - Best things
Schwartzs

Cranberry...

(Greef Diner)

Amy Polchki Review
"Glorified Stoner Food"
—28 Seats does not make
a restaurant.

Picard Peanuts
Tobacco turned to Spanish Peanuts.
only Two producers
left

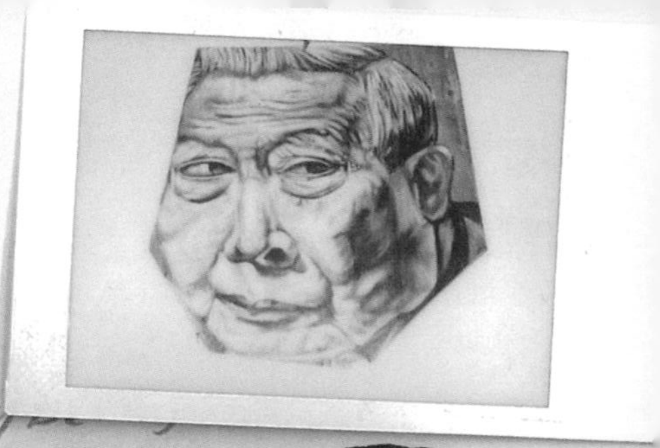

Patty Melt

ST

ST

Chapter 1 The long Road to "Poses and Sons"

A very Serious Restaurant "Canadian Diner"

Tuesday Fat Kid

Test 4 —

Mature Shrimp Cocktail — Dax Hartres

Freezer Moose/Bear Chili —

Wild Leek Garlic Bread - Montpellier Butter -

Crab Fried Rice - "Drives you crazy across
the U.S.A"
House Special Pork Fried Rice - uncle Tung

Brussel Sprout Caesar Salad

Butterscotch Squares - B

Milkshakes
Brownie surprise

WHEN I STARTED SERVING bacon and eggs, the reactions ranged from "What?" and "Crazy!" to "What an idiot." I stuck to my guns and kept going, and then all of a sudden, people were like "Whoa" and "What a genius!" and "Anthony is the best chef I know!!" and "I love Anthony so much!!!" My tombstone will read:

ANTHONY JAMES ROSE
Loving Father, Brother, Son
Tender Lover and Genius Inventor of Bacon and Eggs
May He Rest in Grease

SCHMALTZ HASH:

1 lb	Yukon Gold potatoes
	Vegetable oil, for frying
1/4 cup	duck fat
4 sprigs	fresh thyme, leaves only
2 tsp	duck salt (page 250)
3/4 cup	caramelized onions (page 17)
4 slices	thick-cut bacon
2	hunter sausages or something smoked and delicious (see note)
6 large	eggs
1 Tbsp	unsalted butter
	Kosher salt and freshly ground black pepper
4 slices	thick-cut caraway rye bread or any bread you like
4 Tbsp	finger chili hot sauce (page 251)

1. For the hash, cut your potatoes into thick matchsticks. This is best accomplished using a mandoline with the teeth on it, but you can also use a sharp knife. Just make sure to cut your pieces evenly so they cook evenly. Soak the potatoes in cold water for 30 minutes to pull out most of the starch. Change the water 4 times during this 30 minutes.

2. If you have a deep fryer, fill it with enough vegetable oil so that the potatoes can move around freely, and heat the oil to 345°F. A kitchen thermometer is helpful here. If you don't have a deep fryer, you can use a large Dutch oven or high-sided pot. Line a large plate with paper towels and preheat the oven to 200°F.

3. Blanch the matchstick potatoes for 2 minutes or until they become soft but do not yet take on any color. Using a slotted spoon, transfer them to the paper towel-lined plate to soak up any excess oil.

4. In a large cast-iron pan, heat the duck fat over medium heat. When the potatoes have cooled a bit, transfer them to the pan and add the thyme, duck salt, and caramelized onions. Keep an eye on the potatoes and flip them when they have become golden brown and delicious-y; this should take about 5 to 7 minutes per side. Transfer the potatoes to a baking sheet and keep them warm in the oven while you prepare the rest of the breakfast.

5. Wipe down the cast-iron pan and fry the bacon over medium heat until crispy on both sides, about 3 to 4 minutes per side. Transfer the bacon to the baking sheet in the oven to keep warm. I like to keep the bacon warm right on top of the potatoes. It's like two gods mingling.

6. Split the sausages lengthwise down the middle and fry in the leftover bacon fat for about 5 minutes per side. Since the sausages are already smoked and cooked, we're just looking to crisp them on each side.

7. Fry your eggs in any remaining bacon fat and a good knob of butter. Sunny-side up is best, and remember to season with salt and pepper.

8. Serve with a side of toasted rye bread (or any bread you choose) and finger chili hot sauce.

NOTE: The local suppliers I use are Perth Pork Products for the bacon, Andy's Sausages, and Harbord Bakery for the bread. If you can't find hunter sausages, get ones that are smoked and precooked so you just have to crisp them up.

I CAN EAT ONLY ONE PER YEAR,
BUT THE FAT KID IN ME EATS IT
Every Day.

PATTY MELT

NOT QUITE A HAMBURGER and not quite a grilled cheese, this is a grilled cheese sandwich with a hamburger patty inside. It's the best non-hamburger in Toronto, as voted unanimously by me. The grilled cheese is fried in butter and the burger is fried in butter and the onions are fried in butter. I can eat only one per year, but the fat kid in me eats it every day, breakfast, lunch, and dinner.

CARAMELIZED ONIONS:

2 large	white onions, about 1 lb each
3 Tbsp	canola oil
1 Tbsp	unsalted butter
1 tsp	kosher salt
6 sprigs	fresh thyme
12 pieces	thick-sliced caraway rye bread (about 1 loaf)
1/2 cup	unsalted butter
12 (1 oz)	slices orange or aged white cheddar
2 1/4 lb	freshly ground beef (see note)
	Kosher salt and freshly ground black pepper
	Your favorite condiments, for serving (I like a spicy brown mustard and very little else)

1. Preheat the oven to 250°F.

2. For the caramelized onions, slice the onions thinly and preheat a large pan over medium heat. Add the canola oil and butter to the pan. Once it starts to shimmer, you're ready to fry the onions. Don't worry about crowding the pan; it will work to your advantage. Let the onions start to brown on the bottom, about 3 to 4 minutes, then add the salt and thyme. Mix the onions to let the flavors combine. Leave the onions for another few minutes, then stir. Continue this process until the onions are evenly browned, then remove from the heat. Try not to stir the onions too much; rather, let them sit to really sear between your stirs.

3. Assemble the grilled cheese sandwiches. Butter all 12 slices of the rye bread, then turn half of them butter side down. On the bread side, place two slices of cheddar and a generous heap of the caramelized onions. Close the sandwiches so the butter is on the outsides, and fry in a large pan over medium heat until the sandwiches are golden and the cheese has melted on the inside, about 3 minutes per side. Transfer the sandwiches to a baking sheet and keep them warm in the oven.

4. Divide your ground beef into six evenly sized balls, then flatten them slightly to form patties. Use your thumb to make a small dimple in the center of each patty. Season the patties with salt and pepper.

5. Heat two large frying pans on high heat, and wait for them to come to temperature. They should be very hot. Fry the patties for 2 to 3 minutes per side for medium-rare.

6. Once the burgers are cooked, remove your sandwiches from the oven and open them up—careful, they'll be hot inside! Put a burger patty inside each one, close it up, and cut it in half. Serve with your favorite condiments.

[ROSE AND SONS]

NOTE: I recommend getting your beef from a reliable butcher who grinds meat daily, since these patty melts are best served medium-rare.

JW BIRD

I LOVE JONATHAN WAXMAN SO MUCH. Jonathan is a pioneer of California cuisine, but I first met him when I worked at the Washington Park Restaurant in New York. He has remained one of my greatest mentors as a chef and a good friend to this day. Working with JW really took me to the next level as a chef. The simplicity of his food at Washington Park, paired with impossibly luxurious wines, was an education. This is based on his recipe, except I brine the birds in pickle juice rather than a classic brine. Nevertheless, the technique is all his: slow-grilled and skin side down about 90 percent of the way so it's crispy and holy good, then covered in salsa verde, just as JW taught me. Beyond the bird, I have stolen many a recipe and technique from this great man.

2 whole	Cornish hens or small chickens
Pickle juice	to cover your birds

SALSA VERDE:

1/4 cup	small-diced shallots
1/4 cup	small-diced sour pickles
1/4 cup	chopped capers
1/2 bunch	fresh parsley, chopped
1 bunch	fresh chives, chopped
1 bunch	fresh tarragon, chopped
1/2 bunch	fresh dill, chopped
	Zest of 1/2 lemon
3 cups	olive oil
	Kosher salt and freshly ground black pepper

1. Spatchcock your birds. Lay the birds breast side down and use kitchen shears to cut down each side of the spine. Remove the spine and the wing tips (you can save these for stock), then turn the birds over, press down on the breastbone, and flatten them.

2. Place the birds in a large container with a tight-fitting lid, cover with the pickle juice, and refrigerate. Soak the birds in the juice for 24 to 48 hours, depending on your taste, then remove and dry the birds off with a clean dish towel.

3. Preheat your barbecue on medium heat, then put your flattened birds, skin side down, on the grill. Turn the heat down to low and close the lid. Cook for about 20 minutes without opening the lid of the barbecue. This will make the skin beautiful and crispy. Flip the birds and cook for 2 to 3 minutes, just to let the heat kiss the flesh and bones. Remove the birds from the heat and let them rest for 5 to 10 minutes.

4. Combine all the salsa verde ingredients in a bowl. Taste and adjust seasoning as needed.

5. Once your birds have rested, cut them into eighths. Use a knife that you don't mind cutting through bones with. Separate the drumsticks from the thighs and cut the breasts in half.

6. Arrange your birds on a platter and generously smother them with the salsa verde.

[ROSE AND SONS]

NOTE: Brining your birds for 72 hours creates the most pickly pickle flavor.

CORNBREAD

WHEN I WAS A STUDENT at the California Culinary Academy in the early 90s, Peter Reinhart was an instructor. Peter was, and still is, one of the most highly respected bread bakers in North America. I never took any of his classes, but I picked his brain daily about bagels and beyond. He was so far ahead of the curve and went on to rule the world with his magic. He's written a number of books, but his first one—Brother Juniper's Bread Book: Slow Rise as Method and Metaphor—is my favorite. I use this adapted recipe of his as a base for not only cornbread but also pancakes, hush puppies, muffins, and corn-dog batter.

2 cups	all-purpose flour
3/4 cup	cornmeal
3/4 cup	grits
2 Tbsp	baking powder
2 tsp	kosher salt
1/2 cup + 1 Tbsp	white sugar
1	jalapeño, seeded and diced small
1 cup	shredded cheddar
2	large eggs
1/4 cup	melted unsalted butter
2 1/2 cups	buttermilk
1/4 cup	duck fat or pork lard (see note)

1. Preheat the oven to 350°F and place a 12-inch cast-iron pan inside to get hot.

2. In a large bowl, combine the flour, cornmeal, grits, baking powder, salt, sugar, jalapeños, and cheddar.

3. In a separate bowl, whisk the eggs, melted butter, and buttermilk.

4. Slowly pour the wet ingredients into the dry, and mix gently by hand.

5. Once your batter is ready, take the cast-iron pan out of the oven and add the duck fat to the pan. Move it around so the whole surface gets coated with the fat, including the sides of the pan.

6. Pour the batter into the pan and return to the oven. Bake for 30 minutes, then rotate the pan and bake for another 30 minutes.

7. Remove the pan from the oven. Using a toothpick, poke a hole in the center of the cornbread. If the toothpick comes out clean, you're done. If not, return the pan to the oven for another few minutes, then check again.

8. Let the pan cool for a few minutes, then flip it upside down onto a resting rack to cool completely.

[ROSE AND SONS]

NOTE: You can substitute the duck fat or pork lard with butter or oil. For serving, I like a good drizzle of maple syrup, some hot sauce, a shower of scallions, and a dollop of pimento cheese.

BRUSSELS SPROUT CAESAR

SERVES 2 TO 4

WHENEVER I HIRE A NEW CHEF, we have a brainstorming session at my house to talk food and shoot the shit. When I hired Jesse Grasso at Rose and Sons and we had our brainstorming session, it was mostly bullshit with a little talk of food sprinkled on top. We both wanted to keep the integrity of the classics at R&S, but let Jesse's food join in. This dish was a collaboration and a huge hit from the get-go, and I think that it will be the new standard for all Caesar salads. The Caesar salad originated in Mexico, and I've decided that it's no longer a Tijuana treat, but a Toronto tickle!

CARAWAY CROUTONS:
3 slices	caraway rye bread
1/3 cup	unsalted butter
	Kosher salt

PICKLED RED ONIONS:
1	red onion, thinly sliced
1/2 cup	red wine vinegar
1/2 cup	white sugar
1 tsp	kosher salt

CAESAR DRESSING:
4 cloves	garlic, smashed
1/4 cup	dijon mustard (we use Kozlik's Daily Dijon)
2	egg yolks
1/4 cup	red wine vinegar
1/4 cup	fresh lemon juice
8	salted anchovies, fillets removed from bones
1 cup	canola oil
1 cup	olive oil
1 cup	grated Parmigiano Reggiano
	Kosher salt and freshly ground black pepper
	Tabasco, to taste
	Worcestershire, to taste
	Vegetable oil, for frying
4 cups	brussels sprouts, cleaned and halved
2 cups	brussels sprouts, cleaned and thinly sliced
1/4 cup	finger chili hot sauce (page 251)

1. For the croutons, butter your bread on both sides and fry in a large pan over medium heat until golden brown on both sides, about 1 to 2 minutes per side. Remove the bread from the pan, season with salt, and cut into croutons.

2. For the pickled onions, place the sliced onions in a large bowl. In a small pot, combine the red wine vinegar, sugar, salt, and 1/2 cup water. Bring to a boil, then pour the liquid over the onions and let cool.

3. For the Caesar dressing, combine the garlic, mustard, egg yolks, vinegar, lemon juice, and anchovies in a food processor and process until it's as smooth as you can get it.

4. With the food processor running, slowly drizzle in the canola and olive oils so the dressing can emulsify.

5. Add the grated Parmigiano Reggiano and pulse the food processor until the dressing comes together. Season with salt, pepper, Tabasco, and Worcestershire. Store in a jar until ready to use.

6. To prepare the brussels sprouts, heat the vegetable oil in a deep fryer or large Dutch oven until it reaches 365°F. Use enough oil so that the sprouts can move around freely. Fry only the halved brussels sprouts until soft with some color, about 1 to 2 minutes. Be careful, the sprouts spit a lot when they're in the deep fryer!

7. In a large bowl, mix together the cooked and raw sliced brussels sprouts, croutons, 4 Tbsp pickled onions, 1/3 cup Caesar dressing, and hot sauce to taste. Taste and season with salt if necessary. The remaining onions and dressing can be kept in the fridge for about 1 week and used for sandwiches, salads, or whatever you like.

NOTE: I like serving these vegetables as a side dish alongside a steak. They work great with a grilled JW Bird (page 18) as well.

HOUSE OF CHAN VEGETABLES

ALL MY LONGTIME RESTAURANT LOVES are closing up shop. I like the old and familiar and the comfy, and I yearn for flavors that I grew up with and continue to shove in my mouth. The House of Chan in Toronto reigns supreme and is still here, thank god. My great-uncle Jack was an original partner, along with so many other big machers. Every celebration in my family was held there, and I remember that we ate steak nonstop, with a little lobster and some chicken balls thrown in for good measure. All the steaks came with fried potatoes and crispy onions and a plate of vegetables that you cut up yourself and sprinkled with oil and vinegar from a cruet.

VINAIGRETTE:

1/4 cup	red wine vinegar
2 Tbsp	dijon mustard
1 tsp	kosher salt
3/4	cup olive oil

FRENCH DRESSING:

1/2 cup	vinaigrette (see above)
1/4 cup	ketchup
1 dash	Worcestershire
1 Tbsp	orange juice
1/8 tsp	paprika
1/2 tsp	grated fresh ginger
1 tsp	finely chopped fresh tarragon
1 tsp	finely chopped fresh parsley
6	baby orange carrots, tops attached
6	baby red carrots, tops attached
6	baby yellow carrots, tops attached
About 8	Cincinnati radishes, tops attached (though any other radishes will do)
1 bunch	scallions
1	red onion
25 to 30	heirloom cherry tomatoes
1 head	celery, cut into large sticks, leaves left on the center pieces
1/2 cup	blue cheese dressing (page 252)
1/2 cup	ranch dressing (page 253)

1. For the vinaigrette, combine the red wine vinegar, mustard, salt, and olive oil in a blender and emulsify all the ingredients together. Alternatively, you can whisk by hand, slowly drizzling in the oil.

2. For the french dressing, blend 1/2 cup of the vinaigrette with the ketchup, Worcestershire, orange juice, paprika, ginger, tarragon, and parsley.

3. If any of your vegetables are a bit limp, soak them in ice water for an hour to breathe new life into them.

4. Wash, but don't peel, the carrots and radishes. Scrub them with a clean green scrubber pad to remove the dirt and roots from the outside.

5. Remove the roots and the top inch of the scallions, and peel and cut the red onion into 1/4-inch-thick rings. Soak both types of onion in ice water for about an hour to remove any bitterness.

6. Wash the cherry tomatoes and celery sticks.

7. Arrange all the vegetables on a platter, and transfer the french dressing, blue cheese dressing, and ranch dressing to small individual bowls or jars that will fit in a condiment caddy. You can also chop up all the vegetables for a chopped salad.

[ROSE AND SONS]

BROWNIE SURPRISE

FOR THIS DESSERT, you first need to go out and buy a soft-serve ice-cream machine, which should run you many thousands of dollars. Then make delicious junk foods, and all will be good. Caramel is good by itself and even better with Canadian whisky—it's fine for the kids, because the alcohol burns off and only the sweet, sweet notes of barrel-aged goodness tickle the tongue.

PEANUT BUTTER SAUCE:

1 cup	smooth processed peanut butter (I like Skippy, though it's no longer available in Canada)
1/4 cup	canola oil
1/2 cup	icing sugar
1/4 tsp	kosher salt

CHOCOLATE SYRUP
(OR SUBSTITUTE U-BET ORIGINAL
CHOCOLATE FLAVOR SYRUP):

3/4 cup	white sugar
1 cup	cocoa powder
1 1/2 tsp	vanilla
1/2 tsp	kosher salt

BROWN-BUTTER CARAMEL SAUCE:

1/2 cup	unsalted butter
1 cup	heavy cream (35%)
1 1/4 cups	brown sugar
1 tsp	kosher salt
1 tsp	vanilla extract
2 Tbsp	whisky
1	large brownie, homemade or store-bought
1 1/2 cups	soft-serve or regular vanilla ice cream (you can also go to Dairy Queen)
1/4 cup	Ontario red-skinned peanuts or any good peanuts

1. Preheat the oven to 350°F and line a baking sheet with parchment paper.

2. For the peanut butter sauce, combine the peanut butter, canola oil, icing sugar, and salt in a food processor and process until smooth.

3. For the chocolate syrup, combine the sugar and 2 cups of water in a large pot. Bring to a boil, then reduce to a simmer and add the cocoa powder. Whisk until the mixture has thickened and is smooth. Stir in the vanilla and salt, then pass the sauce through a fine-mesh sieve to remove any lumps. Cool and store in a jar.

4. For the caramel sauce, in a medium pot over low heat, melt the butter and allow it to start turning brown. Keep your eyes on it so it doesn't burn. Once the color has started to change, remove from heat and slowly add in the cream. Add the brown sugar, salt, vanilla, and whisky and return the pot to the heat. Gently bring up to a boil, and stir to make sure the sugar has melted. Remove from heat and cool the sauce in the pot or in a metal container before transferring to a jar.

5. Cut your brownie in half and open it up like a sandwich. Place it on the baking sheet and heat in the preheated oven for 4 to 5 minutes or until hot.

6. Transfer the brownie to a plate or bowl and cover with the ice cream, 2 Tbsp of each sauce, and the peanuts.

NOTE: My all-time favorite ice cream is Peanut Butter 'N Chocolate from Baskin Robbins. My son, Simon, and I can polish off many a pint very quickly. And it is always a great choice for this dessert if you don't want to buy a soft-serve machine.

ROOT BEER AND BOURBON COCKTAIL

I'M NOT A COCKTAIL PERSON AT ALL, but I came up with this recipe all by myself. The truth is that I was really just trying to be as lazy as possible, so I put together a couple of things that I drink a lot. It actually worked and it worked well. You can make this with bourbon or Canadian whisky. I prefer it with rye, but it sounds so much better as "Root Beer and Bourbon." Just rrrrrrrrolls off the tongue. Try it! Ha, you did.

	Ice
1 oz	Canadian rye or bourbon
1 bottle	good-quality root beer (I like Stewart's, IBC, or A&W)
2 splashes	blackstrap bitters
1	maraschino cherry

1. Fill a 10 oz rocks glass with ice.

2. Pour the rye or bourbon over the ice and top with root beer and the blackstrap bitters.

3. Garnish with a maraschino cherry.

Flask Whiskey Cocktails

ROSE AND SONS CAESAR: A CANADIAN COCKTAIL

IN THE PAST FIVE YEARS, almost six years by the time you read this infamous tome, we have served over one million brunches at Rose and Sons. This is a pretty classic recipe, other than the quality of the Caesar juice mix. We use Walter, a local brand that makes it seem like you're drinking sunshine with vodka and Tabasco. And, in much the same way as you wouldn't wear white after Labor Day, I would advise that you not drink this past 3 pm, or you will die.

	Duck salt, enough to rim the glass (page 250)
	Ice
1 oz	vodka, or more to taste (I like it with more)
4 oz	Walter Caesar mix
1 tsp	prepared horseradish, or more or less to taste (I like it with more)
3 splashes	Tabasco, or more or less to taste (I like it with more)
2 splashes	Worcestershire (no more!)
1/4	lime
1/2	sour pickle

1. Rim a 10 oz rocks glass with duck salt, then fill it to the top with ice.

2. Pour the vodka over the ice and top with the Walter Caesar mix.

3. Add the horseradish, Tabasco, and Worcestershire and stir.

4. Garnish with the lime and sour pickle.

[ROSE AND SONS]

NOTE: I actually prefer my Caesar chilled, without ice. If you'd like to make it that way, prepare the drink over the ice in a separate glass or cocktail shaker, then strain it into the rocks glass rimmed with duck salt.

BIG CROW

GARLIC BREAD | 40

GRILLED LOBSTER | 43

POKE-ISH | 44

RIB ROAST | 47

COWBOY ONIONS | 48

BAKED POTATO EXTRA VAGANZA (2 WORDS) | 51

PICKLE PLATE | 52

WARM S'MORES CAKE | 55

BOHEMIAN COOLER COCKTAIL | 56

-28 Seats does not make a restacrant.

TWO COOKS PARADE A WHOLE ROASTED PIG through the dining room as though it's an old-timey duchess being transported to her rendezvous in a grand sedan chair. It's a scene that happens quite a bit when you hang out with Anthony, actually, and it never gets old.

The timelessness of the moment, a Renaissance painting come to life, is only enhanced by the smell of woodsmoke from the massive grill, the sound of a guitar being strummed, and the abundance of animal hides strewn across the rough-hewn benches.

We're at Big Crow, the backyard barbecue joint set discreetly behind Rose and Sons. It's Anthony's most elemental and, in some ways, his most loved restaurant. It was also never supposed to happen.

"When we took over People's Foods, there were still tenants living in the house upstairs," Anthony recalls. "As they moved out we took over. The backyard where Big Crow is now was just a backyard. It was never meant to be its own restaurant, but operating a 28-seat diner is insane, so we wanted to find a way to bring more people in."

At first, the idea was just to cook the food in Rose and Sons and move it to the backyard, but Anthony and his team quickly realized that the distance was too far and too awkward, so they moved a little grill out back to cook off of. From there, it snowballed.

The idea of creating a Southern barbecue joint was floated briefly, but Anthony had been burnt by that particular genre once before. "It's harsh out there for a barbecue joint," he says. "Purists are so judgy. Even when I opened Drake BBQ, which was just pulled pork and brisket, I heard the same two things: 'Oh, they don't serve chopped brisket in Texas' and 'This sauce isn't how it's supposed to be.' Barbecue people are tough."

As Big Crow's simple wooden walls went up and the shipping container that would serve as the bar and prep kitchen was settled into place, the space took on a kind of Quebec sugar shack meets Ontario cottage vibe. Being in a back-yard automatically brought up memories of being in the country and cooking outside. Clearly, the evocation of barbecue was not going away, so Anthony decided to simply draw inspiration from Canadian backyard barbecues, a style with fewer rigid rules and more room to include all kinds of traditions.

With the concept in place, the cooks were free to play with ideas; everything from peameal bacon subs and chopped brisket nachos to Cornish hens brined in pickle juice and smoked ox tongue. Even whole hogs roasted in a La Caja China, a Chinese/Cuban contraption that cooks a pig in a box beneath a pile of coals. That same China Box, as they're known, is where tonight's epic beast comes from. The tawny, 80-pound hog is the centerpiece for a meal Anthony is hosting for the crew behind the Boots and Hearts Music Festival.

"Of all the music events we've catered over the years—WayHome, Field Trip, NXNE—Boots and Hearts was always my favorite," Anthony says. "Nobody loves music like country-music fans."

On a big table just outside the dining room, there are a whole bed's worth of oysters, lined up waiting to be shucked: sweet Beausoleils from New Brunswick; plump, firm French Hooters from PEI; rich Tatamagouches from Nova Scotia.

"This is my first," announces Mark, a bulky stagehand who is about to pop his oyster cherry. He tilts the shell back, winces, and immediately chases the bivalve with a slug of beer. "How was it?" I ask. "Not bad," he says through watering eyes. Cold, saline, and with a cucumber sweetness, they taste much better than "not bad" to me.

I polish off a few more and head inside just in time to hear Stan Dunford, the legendary venture capitalist, transportation executive, and founder of Boots and Hearts, introduce tonight's performer, a musician named Jesse Gold whom Stan discovered as part of the festival's emerging artist showcase series. Decked out head to toe in black and looking a bit like a hip, bearded Hank Williams, Jesse launches into an impressive acoustic set, just a singer and a guitar, of blue-eyed country soul.

A table of fans sway to the music and sing along with every word, positioning themselves to make sure Jesse is framed in the background of their peace-sign-flashing selfies.

After the final chord is strummed and the applause dies down, it's time to eat. The cooks—Anthony included—have been busily reducing the hog to a pile of shreds and shards of crisp skin. As the plates start to arrive, people squeeze together along the long rows of benches to make room for their friends and slather gamey whipped duck fat over slices of dark, heavy bread. Crisp tortillas are dragged through creamy guacamole. Even the salad gets a turn on the grill, imbuing the romaine and treviso with a dose of smoke. Meat plates arrive, pulled pork, of course, but also thick sausage links and caramelized chicken, and with them more flavor in the form of squeeze bottles full of sauce: earthy and rich chopped mushroom salsa, grilled wild leek relish made with leeks from around Anthony's cottage, and jalapeño cream.

In the midst of the feasting, I catch a glimpse of Anthony standing alone in a quiet corner, surveying the scene. Wiping the pork fat off my face, I excuse myself and walk over. "Happy with the party?" I ask.

"Totally," he says. "You know, what I love about this place is that it kind of just came into its own. We didn't want to push anything on the restaurant. We wanted it to evolve into what it wanted to be. You can't create culture."

GARLIC BREAD

AS A GOOD JEWISH KID GROWING UP IN TORONTO, I frequented the Steak Pit. The Steak Pit was the best worst steak house ever, though they were somehow famous for their Mexican Ribs. Anyhoo, all meals would come with garlic bread on a baguette with loads of butter, wrapped in the cheapest polyester napkin ever. This is nothing like that. With three cheeses and butter and smoke and a grill, this is so far away from the Steak Pit, it's crazy, but that's exactly where the inspiration for this recipe comes from.

GARLIC BUTTER:

1 cup	unsalted butter
About 14	cloves garlic, peeled

HERB BUTTER:

1 bunch	fresh thyme
1 bunch	fresh rosemary
1/2 cup	unsalted butter
1/2 bunch	chopped fresh parsley
1	baguette
2 tsp	duck salt (page 250)
1 1/4 cups + 1 Tbsp	shredded smoked mozzarella, cheddar, or monterey jack (could be a mix of all three, or just one if that's all ya got)

1. For the garlic butter, combine the butter and garlic in a medium pot on low heat. Cook until the garlic is super-soft and has a bit of color, about 25 to 30 minutes, then put in a bowl in the fridge to cool.

2. For the herb butter, tie your thyme and rosemary together with a piece of butcher's twine to make a brush out of the leaves. Melt the 1/2 cup butter in a pot with the herb brush sitting in it to infuse the flavors. Turn the heat off once the butter has melted, but leave the herb brush sitting in the pot.

3. Preheat the oven to 350°F.

4. Once the herb butter has cooled and has started to firm up a bit, add the garlic butter and parsley and mix well to combine the flavors.

5. Split the baguette down one side and open it up like a sandwich.

6. Spread a healthy amount of garlic-herb butter down both sides of the bread, season with duck salt, and stuff with all of the cheeses (or just the one cheese, if that's what you're using).

7. Close your baguette, cut it in half, and wrap it in aluminum foil.

8. At the restaurants, we heat up the garlic bread in the smoker to make it extra-delicious, but if you don't have a smoker, just bake it in the preheated oven for about 20 minutes.

9. Turn on your barbecue when the garlic bread goes in the oven or smoker.

10. Once the garlic bread is melty in the middle, take it out of the foil and grill it on the barbecue to get some char on the outside. Watch it closely, as this should take only a minute or two. If you have something to weigh it down with, that will make the bread perfectly crispy and smooshy all at the same time.

11. When the garlic bread is done grilling, butter both sides with the herb brush and sprinkle with a little extra duck salt.

12. Cut the loaf into fingers and serve. Any remaining garlic-herb butter can be kept in the fridge or shaped into a log and frozen.

NOTE: We have served this with black truffles smothered inside, to lovely results. You could also include brisket and/or chopped pork inside to make it a sandwich.

[BIG CROW]

Flask Whisked Cocktails

Maple Candy Or Snow
Beaver Tail - Soft Serve

1000 island Dressing
pecan toasted / 1000 island Dressing

Snow Story of Camping Growing up, Camp, Cottage, All song time, 1C maga hi

Canadian BBQ vs Southern BBQ

pre Lunch
"Fat Buck-east" to rural. Th

BARRELHOUSE
MAMAS
Born in the Alley, Raised up in the slum
Classic Piano Rags, Blues
and Stomp from the

Lumberjack Breakfast - Comes from lumberjack history

W: 10/Blueberry Jam
Bacon - Braised-Smoked PorkBelly
Schmitz Hash
Eggs - Soft and Sexy
Buck wheat Pancakes - Farm On
Sausage -

Peameal/Bacon-vs-Canadian Bacon

Peameal/Sawdust

Split Pea Soup

Sugar Shack
Brinsing/North South
Big Crow Lame Story

L. Jensinn
- Michaela Jolerja

Top ten Surviable / Tips
Forties -

ABTRX

GRILLED LOBSTER

I LIKE A 2 LB LOBSTER TO MYSELF with butter and a squeeze of lemon, and I don't like to share it at all—okay, maybe with my beautiful son, Simon, but just maybe. Moving on: Montpelier butter is one of those impossibly amazing recipes from Jeremiah Tower. Other than that, I don't know where it comes from. I do know, though, that I like as much butter as I can get on my lobster—so much that it drips down my arm as I bring the lobster to my mouth. Just like JT does when he butters his blinis. So you could say we are the same.

	Kosher salt
2	whole (2 lb) lobsters
1/4 cup	olive oil
	Montpelier butter, for serving (page 256)
	Lemon wedges, for serving

1. Preheat your barbecue to medium-high, and bring a large pot of generously salted water to a boil over high heat—you should use about 2 Tbsp kosher salt per 4 cups water. The pot should be big enough to fit both your lobsters.

2. Once the water has boiled, drop your lobsters in and let them cook for 6 minutes.

3. With a pair of tongs, remove the lobsters and let them cool for about 10 minutes.

4. Remove the rubber bands from the claws, and cut the lobsters in half lengthwise. To do this, use an old knife you don't care about or heavy kitchen shears.

5. Rub a bit of olive oil on the lobster flesh and sprinkle with salt.

6. Place the lobsters, flesh side down, on the hot barbecue for 3 to 4 minutes to get some good char on them.

7. Courtesy-crack the claws open, and put a healthy amount of Montpelier butter on top, or serve it melted on the side. Serve with lemon wedges.

[BIG CROW]

POKE-ISH

THIS IS NOT POKE AT ALL, not even close—but kinda sorta. It's more like a salmon tartare on tortilla chips but with some Asian flavors and peanuts. I love peanuts so much. Did you know that Ontario has the best peanuts in the world? You see, years ago, the local government took away all the subsidies from tobacco farmers, but lo and behold, the same great soil used for tobacco also grows incredible Spanish red-skinned peanuts! The rest is history—not like a crazy lucrative history, as there are only like three growers left, but history nonetheless.

	Vegetable oil, for frying (optional)
12	large yellow corn tortillas, or really good tortilla chips
12 oz	sushi-grade salmon fillet, bones and skin removed
1/4 cup	finely chopped red onions
1/2 cup	finely chopped scallions
1/2 cup	chopped fresh cilantro + few sprigs for garnish
4 Tbsp	Ontario red-skinned peanuts
1 Tbsp	furikake (can be found at Asian grocery stores)
1	lime, cut into wedges

POKE DRESSING:

3 Tbsp	chopped pickled ginger
1/4 cup	rice wine vinegar
2 Tbsp	maple syrup
1 Tbsp	soy sauce
1 tsp	chili flakes
1/4 cup	olive oil
1/4 cup	canola oil
3 dashes	Tabasco

1. If you'd like to make your own tortilla chips, prepare your deep fryer and heat the vegetable oil to 365°F. Use enough oil so that the tortillas can move around freely. Cut each of your fresh corn tortillas into six wedges and fry until golden and crispy, about 3 to 4 minutes. When the sizzling sound stops, you'll know that all the moisture has gone and the chips are ready. If you aren't going to fry your own tortillas, get some that are freshly made. (In Toronto, I recommend going to La Tortilleria.)

2. Cut your salmon into long strips, then dice the fish into 1/2-inch cubes.

3. For the poke dressing, combine the pickled ginger, rice wine vinegar, maple syrup, and soy sauce in a blender and puree for 1 minute.

4. Add the chili flakes, olive oil, canola oil, and Tabasco and blend on low until well incorporated.

5. Toss the salmon with red onions, scallions, cilantro, and about 1/3 cup dressing (you can add more dressing if you like).

6. Evenly spread the salmon poke over the tortilla chips and garnish with peanuts, furikake, lime wedges, and a few sprigs of cilantro.

[BIG CROW]

NOTE: This method works with all big chunky steaks.

RIB ROAST

MY MOM HATES A RIB STEAK (too fatty), but the rest of the family loves it
(so fatty). Steaks are one thing, but slow-roasting a whole or even a half
bone-in roast to rare is the best. Cut it into huge bone-in steaks and rip-roar
till awesomeness bleeds out of every pore. Drizzle some whisky overtop, then drink
more whisky. A little duck salt and marinating in Canadian whisky for a few days
are delightful ideas too. Massage, massage, massage and you're good to go.
Drink more whisky.

4 lb	bone-in rib roast (ask your butcher for the fatty side if you can get it!)
6 Tbsp	Lot No. 40 whisky or whatever your flavor is
2 Tbsp	duck salt (page 250)
1 Tbsp	freshly ground black pepper

1. Create a marinade for your meat. Combine the rib roast with the whisky, duck salt, and pepper and refrigerate for a few days, or overnight.

2. Bring the rib roast out of the fridge and let it sit at room temperature for about 2 hours before cooking.

3. Preheat the oven to 325°F.

4. Put the roast on a baking sheet and place in the preheated oven. It should take about 1 hour to get to rare, but definitely use a meat thermometer and remove the roast from the oven when the internal temperature reaches 110°F. Let the roast stand for about 20 minutes before cutting into it.

5. Using a long knife, remove the meat from the bones and slice the meat. Divide the bones between your guests.

[BIG CROW]

COWBOY ONIONS

I REFERENCE MARK FRANZ many times throughout this book. Mark was the chef at Stars in San Francisco for all of its life. I met Mark at Bradley Ogden's Lark Creek Inn and then was lucky enough to help open Farallon in San Francisco. To this day, he's still one of the greatest chefs and has one of the best palates of anyone I've ever worked with. This dish truly captures that high/low aesthetic I adore. Lowly onions are cooked in the coals, drizzled with whisky, then served next to a glorious rib eye or even with foie gras or lobster. It's very elegant, but also very dirty.

4	large Spanish onions
1	cup whisky (we use Lot No. 40)
4 tsp	duck salt (page 250)
1 bunch	fresh sage, leaves removed
4	bay leaves
8 cloves	garlic, sliced

1. Preheat your barbecue to high, or if you happen to be camping outdoors, prepare your cooking fire.

2. Peel the onions and cut the tops off each, but leave the roots intact. Carefully cut each onion into eighths, but stop cutting about 1 inch above the root. At the end, you should have eight segments per onion, still attached to the root at the bottom.

3. Put the onions on a large sheet of aluminum foil and season the open end of each onion with 3 Tbsp whisky and 1 tsp duck salt. Stuff a few sage leaves, one bay leaf, and two cloves garlic in each onion. Make sure to get the herbs right down into the slices of the onion.

4. Wrap the onions tightly in the foil and throw directly on the barbecue or into the hot coals. Cook for 20 to 30 minutes, turning regularly. Don't be afraid of burning, as you'll remove the charred bits after.

5. When the onions are done, open the packets and remove any charred bits. Finish with the remaining whisky, which you can flambé tableside, if you like.

NOTE: I use Duck Salt in many places, both in this book and in my personal life. It is one more perfect thing I picked up from Mark.

[BIG CROW]

NOTE: We use salmon roe and wasabi tobiko here, but feel free to ball out with some sturgeon caviar.

BAKED POTATO EXTRA VAGANZA (2 WORDS)

SERVES 6

LESS IS MORE; keep it simple. Except when it comes to baked potatoes, when more is more and simple is fucked. The best baked potatoes come from steakhouses, and two of my favorites are located in Montreal: Moishes and Gibbys. I love them both, but I remember the baked potato service at Gibbys as pure perfection. The more I could put on that spud, the better, and the garnishes were overflowing. How much garnish did I put on? If I could still see the potato, there was not enough on it.

6	large Yukon Gold or baking potatoes
1/2 cup	vegetable oil
	Kosher salt and freshly ground black pepper
1 cup	sour cream
2 cups	shredded cheddar
1 lb	bacon, fried until very crispy
4	scallions, thinly sliced on a bias
1/2 cup	salmon roe or wasabi tobiko (see note)
1/2 cup	finely grated fresh horseradish

1. Preheat your oven to 350°F and line a baking sheet with aluminum foil.

2. Wash your potatoes and poke them all over with a fork. This will stop them from exploding from the pressure. Toss your taters with some oil, salt, and pepper and wrap them individually with aluminum foil. Place on the baking sheet and bake for 30 minutes, then turn over and bake for another 30 minutes.

3. Once the potatoes are baked, cut through the foil and into each potato about 1 inch deep, from side to side and from end to end. You'll end up with a cross.

4. Using a dish towel to hold it, squeeze each potato from both ends until it pops open and fluffs up. This will let all of your fillings get everywhere inside your potato.

5. Garnish the potatoes with sour cream, cheddar, bacon, scallions, caviar, and horseradish—and even more things if you want! I love the idea of interactive food here, so I like to set up all the garnishes in bowls for the guests to load their own towers of potato power.

[BIG CROW]

PICKLE PLATE

IN NEW YORK AND JEWISH DELI TERMINOLOGY, a full-sour kosher dill is one that has fully fermented, while a half-sour, which has had a shorter stay in the brine, is still crisp and bright green. Elsewhere, these pickles may sometimes be termed "old" and "new" dills. I lived around the corner from Guss' Pickles in New York, and it was always such a trip to see all those barrels on the streets of the Lower East Side. The best shopping/eating day ever would be Guss', Prune, Katz's, Yonah Schimmel Knish Bakery, and Doughnut Plant, in that order. It seems like a lot because it is.

PICKLED RED PEPPERS:

2	red bell peppers
1 cup	white vinegar
1 cup	white sugar
1/2 Tbsp	kosher salt
4	full-sour pickles
4	half-sour pickles
4	pickled green tomatoes
1 cup	sauerkraut

1. For the pickled red peppers, cut the peppers in half and remove the stems and seeds, then slice into thin strips and place in a large bowl.

2. In a medium pot, combine the vinegar, sugar, and salt with 1 cup water. Bring to a boil, then remove from the heat and pour over the pepper strips. Let this hang out for an hour at room temperature, then taste to see how you like it. Adjust seasoning as needed.

3. Cut your full- and half-sour pickles into 1/2-inch-thick rounds and arrange on a large platter.

4. Cut the tomatoes into quarters, add them to the platter, and make two nice piles of the sauerkraut and peppers.

NOTE: At the restaurants, we make the pickled red peppers in vacuum-pack bags. To do this, cut the liquid ingredients in half and combine all together in the vacuum-pack bags. If you have a vacuum sealer, you can seal the bags, but make sure to let the peppers hang out for an hour before using, as they'll have a better texture this way. As for the other pickles, we get most of ours from Tymek's Natural Foods in Etobicoke, Ontario. They're the real deal, and if you live anywhere nearby, you need to get their pickles.

[BIG CROW]

I'M NOT SAYING

I don't like

S'mores

I JUST DON'T CARE FOR
THE WHOLE SCENARIO.

WARM S'MORES CAKE

HAVE YOU EVER made s'mores by the fire with a dozen or more kids? Napkins galore, burnt and flaming marshmallows, sticky fingers, and screaming children for an hour after that! It would warm my heart, as long as it had nothing to do with me. I'm not saying I don't like s'mores, but I just don't care for the whole scenario. This rendition, I promise you, is way better.

1 cup	unsalted butter, room temperature, + extra to grease the pan
2 cups	white sugar
5	large eggs
1 cup	buttermilk
4 cups	graham cracker crumbs
4 Tbsp	baking powder
1 tsp	kosher salt
1 cup	chocolate chips + extra for garnish
1 cup	mini marshmallows + extra for garnish

1. Preheat the oven to 350°F.

2. In a stand mixer, cream together the butter and sugar until fluffy, about 5 minutes.

3. With the mixer running at medium speed, add the eggs, one at a time, until fully combined.

4. With the mixer on low, add the buttermilk, graham cracker crumbs, baking powder, and salt. Mix on low until everything is combined.

5. Using a spatula, fold in the chocolate chips and marshmallows.

6. Grease the inside of a 10-inch springform pan with butter, lard, or cooking spray, and line the bottom with parchment paper.

7. Pour the batter into the pan and use your spatula to make sure it's evenly distributed.

8. Bake for 45 to 60 minutes, then check the center with a toothpick to make sure it's fully cooked. If it comes out clean, you're good to go. If not, return it to the oven for a few more minutes and check again.

9. This is great with melted chocolate poured overtop and blowtorched marshmallows.

[BIG CROW]

BOHEMIAN COOLER COCKTAIL

SERVES 1

THIS IS BY FAR the greatest-selling cocktail of all time at Big Crow. The dichotomy of drinking a super-sexy and extremely sophisticated cocktail while sucking Alabama barbecue sauce gently off your lover's fingers is brilliant. If I do say so myself.

	Ice
1 1/2 oz	Canadian whisky
1/2 oz	elderflower liqueur
	(I like St-Germain)
1 oz	fresh lemon juice
3 oz	good spicy Caribbean
	ginger beer

1. Fill a 10 oz rocks glass with ice.

2. Pour the whisky into the glass, followed by the elderflower liqueur and lemon juice, and top with the ginger beer. Stir and serve.

"Everyday is the Sabbath"
"Every Friday is the last Supper"

FAT PASHA

"SHABBAT SHALOM," Anthony says, handing me a yarmulke.

"Shabbat shalom," I reply.

I always thought I'd make an excellent Jew—I like books and kvetching and a nice kugel—and the snug way this yarmulke fits just confirms my suspicion.

Anthony's hosting a Friday-night Shabbat (also called Shabbas, in Yiddish) dinner for a few friends and family tonight on the verdant little patio behind his restaurant Fat Pasha. It's no coincidence that we've all gathered here. Fat Pasha is perhaps the most personal of Anthony's restaurants, the one most closely associated with the foods he grew up eating and, therefore, the one that hits closest to home. It might also be the restaurant he was destined to run.

"Fat Pasha was the first restaurant that came looking for us," he says. "It was the legendary Indian Rice Factory for over 40 years, so it had a great history, and the owner, Aman Patel, was a fan of ours. He lived nearby, and we were talking one day and he said, 'You should do something there,' so Rob and I went over, and right away we loved it. It had the patio. It was easy. The only thing was, we didn't have a clue what we were going to do. We just knew we had this wicked space."

Anthony immersed himself in cookbooks to find inspiration. Yotam Ottolenghi was dominating the cookbook shelves at the time—as he still does—with his version of Israeli cooking. The book struck a chord, and Anthony decided this was what the restaurant would be about.

"I forgot one thing, though," he says. "As a Jew in North America, you don't grow up with that food. We grew up with Ashkenazi food: latkes, challah, brisket. I mean, I'd made hummus once or twice, but I'd never made a shakshouka, for example. I'd played with some of those ingredients, but didn't really know them. When I finally realized we could include the Ashkenazi in there too, it was like the whole thing started to make sense."

From the start, Fat Pasha was a hit. The city was hungry for a modern take on Middle Eastern food: latkes cooked in duck schmaltz, rapini and wheat berry tabbouleh, Israeli sufganiyot doughnuts filled with dulce de leche. Alongside the updated twists on dishes, the menu also displayed more classical choices: falafel, fattoush, hummus. Mixing and matching from that menu, it turns out, makes for a pretty traditional and exceptionally delicious Shabbat meal.

The late-summer sun dapples through the leafy garden that surrounds Fat Pasha's patio. Steely Dan plays over the stereo. Anthony's mother, Linda, brought her tablecloths and silver candlesticks from home. Food writer Bonnie Stern, a longtime friend of the family, provided the recipe for the challah that plays a central role in tonight's meal. She has also literally written a book on Friday-night dinners, so she brings some pretty serious expertise on the subject to the table.

When everyone is settled with a white negroni in hand, Anthony gives a little introduction.

"The idea for tonight," he says, "is that I want to recreate my Sabbath that I grew up with at home with my beautiful mother over here and my gorgeous father. These are her candlesticks and prayer book, and her kiddush cup and the seven-year-old Manischewitz. Mom, you can get us started with whatever it is we do."

"We drink a lot first," Linda says, slaying the room.

"No, the first thing we do is light the candles," she continues. When the candles are lit, she sings a blessing: "Baruch a-tah Ado-nai…"

"Good Shabbas, everyone," she says when the prayer is over, then announces: "The Rose tradition after the candles is everyone kisses everyone."

Much double-cheek kissing ensues.

Next, we all take a sip of Manischewitz, my first. "It tastes like Welch's grape juice," I say. A common assessment, it turns out. After, Bonnie and her husband, Raymond, break the challah. Then, and this comes as a bit of a surprise, they toss it around the table. "It's tradition," someone explains. "You didn't know? This is a no-holds-barred Shabbas."

With the formalities out of the way, it's time to eat.

Sharp plates of pickles arrive along with butter-smooth hummus, bowls of blistered little cherry tomatoes with slices of garlic, smoky chopped eggplant with tahini, muhammara (Syrian chili sauce) with toasted walnut breadcrumbs, garlic labneh (creamy cheese) with za'atar (herb and spice mix), and matboucha (like an Israeli salsa) with cranberry beans and smoked paprika.

"We don't eat like this at Shabbas," one of the guests exclaims.

It's also my first time trying gefilte fish, and having heard nothing but horror stories about it, I prepare for the worst. Miracle of miracles, it turns out to be delicious. Smooth and smoky and just the right amount of salty.

A plate of crisp, dark little latkes with sides of applesauce and sour cream is delivered. "That's the apex of Jewish cuisine right there," the lawyer sitting next to me asserts. Anthony's version, extra-crisp and toasty, makes me think they might just be the apex of all cuisine. Here comes the cauliflower—the whole roasted head all covered in sauces, a steak knife jammed in its top, always turns heads (see page 87).

Anthony's now mixing up a bowl of something tasty: caramelized onions and radishes, boiled eggs, crisp chicken skin, and smooth pureed liver. "This is the chopped liver recipe they serve at Sammy's Roumanian in New York," he explains, "the greatest restaurant in the world. There's no better version, so this is the one we serve." I start out spreading it on challah, but am soon eating it by the spoonful. In fact, like everybody else, I've eaten so much that when Anthony announces he's kiboshing the roasted half chicken and grilled salmon with leek relish he had planned to serve, it comes as something of a relief to the stuffed guests.

This is a common problem at Jewish family events, I gather. Rosh Hashanah, Passover Seder, Purim—the results are the same. Everyone fills up so much on the first courses that no one has room for all the mains, of which there are many. Oy vey.

Anthony checks to see if I just want a taste of the salmon or a small piece of chicken.

I demur. "Anthony," I say, "this dinner, this gathering, everything was geshmak. Mazels."

NOTE: You can use half whole wheat flour and half all-purpose, if you like.

BONNIE'S CHALLAH

MAKES 1 VERY LARGE OR 2 MEDIUM-LARGE CHALLAHS

BONNIE STERN IS A CANADIAN CULINARY HERO. And she's fond of saying that she knew me before I was born, because she taught my pregnant mother at her cooking school. Bonnie has guided me since day one, and I owe so much of my career to her generosity and help along the way. We have cooked at the Beard House together and have sat on the same panels to discuss Jewish cookery and its heritage. She has even brought her good friend Yotam Ottolenghi to Rose and Sons, where he loved my bread pudding so much, he adapted it for one of his books. So I've got that going for me. I make so many things that have Bonnie's history attached, including her challah recipe, which she was willing to share. Thank you, Bonnie, with all my heart.

CHALLAH DOUGH:

5 to 6 cups	all-purpose flour, divided, + more if necessary (see note)
1 Tbsp	kosher salt
1/3 cup	white sugar
1 Tbsp	instant yeast (or one 1/4-ounce package)
4	large eggs
1 cup	water, room temperature
1/2 cup + 1 Tbsp	extra virgin olive oil, divided

TOPPING:

2 Tbsp	sesame, poppy, nigella, flax, or sunflower seeds (or a combination, 2 Tbsp in total)

1. For the dough, in a large bowl, combine 3 cups flour with the salt, sugar, and yeast. Whisk the ingredients for 30 seconds to combine evenly.

2. In another bowl, whisk the eggs. Remove and refrigerate 2 Tbsp to use as egg wash for the topping. Whisk the water and 1/2 cup of olive oil into the remaining eggs.

3. Using a wooden spoon, stir the liquid ingredients into the dry ingredients. The dough will be very sticky. Stir in 1 more cup of flour. The dough will still be sticky. Stir in additional flour (1/2 cup to 1 cup) until dough is too stiff to continue stirring. The dough will probably still be sticky.

4. Sprinkle 1/4 cup flour on your work surface. Turn the dough out onto the flour. Using the heels of your hands, knead in enough flour so that the dough doesn't stick to your hands but is still moist. (I usually use almost 6 cups flour in total, but this can vary.) The kneading can also be done in a stand mixer with the dough hook. Knead for about 10 minutes by hand or 5 to 6 minutes in a mixer, until the dough becomes smooth and elastic. Don't worry. Add extra flour gradually, but remember that it's always better to have a slightly soft, moist dough than a hard, dry one—it's more difficult to add liquid to a dry dough than flour to a moist one.

5. Oil a 4-quart bowl with 1 Tbsp olive oil. Place the dough in the bowl and turn the dough over to oil it on all sides. Cover the bowl with plastic wrap and then with a clean dish towel. Let the dough rise until it has doubled, 1 to 2 hours. If you use a 4-quart bowl, the dough should fill the bowl.

6. Once the dough has risen, gently punch it down to release the air, then knead it again to form a ball. There are many ways to shape challah. This will make one really large or two medium-large breads. I usually make two. To do that, divide the dough in half. Then divide each half into thirds and braid them like you would braid hair.

7. You can bake these on baking sheets or in large loaf pans, but make sure that you line either with parchment paper. Transfer the braided challahs to the prepared sheets. Cover each one loosely with oiled plastic wrap and let them rise for 30 to 60 minutes, or until doubled. This is a good time to preheat your oven to 350°F.

8. Once the challahs have risen a second time, brush each one gently with the reserved beaten egg. Sprinkle with seeds. You can combine the seeds or sprinkle sections of the bread with different seeds.

9. Bake in the preheated oven for 20 minutes. Check the bread, and if it's browning too much, lower the oven to 325°F and cover the bread loosely with aluminum foil. Bake 15 to 20 minutes longer, until a meat thermometer inserted into the middle of the bread reaches 185°F to 195°F. If you're making one large challah, it will take longer to bake. Remove bread from pan(s) and cool on a wire rack.

SALATIM

I HADN'T BEEN TO ISRAEL since my bar mitzvah, but went recently for my niece Noa's bat mitzvah with the whole Rose and Offman clans. The food went way beyond my expectations. I loved how, at the beginning of the meal, the servers would come to the table with all these little dishes of salatim and hummus and pitas, then just keep them coming throughout. These salatim are good starters, but if you want to make them into a whole meal, add olives, pickles, tuna salad—whatever you want, really.

BURNT EGGPLANT DIP:

2	medium eggplants, peeled, or leave some skin for texture
1 tsp	kosher salt + extra for seasoning eggplants
	Canola oil, for grilling
1/2 cup	garlic fried tomatoes (page 71)
1 1/2 Tbsp	fresh lemon juice
2 Tbsp	olive oil + extra for garnish
1/3 cup	tahini

1. Preheat the barbecue to high. Slice each eggplant lengthwise into four pieces. Season each piece with salt and rub some canola oil into the flesh.

2. Grill the eggplants on the barbecue until black on both sides. Put all the pieces aside in a bowl to cool down a bit.

3. Chop the eggplants into 1-inch cubes and place in a stand mixer along with any juices that were released.

4. Add the tomatoes, lemon juice, olive oil, and tahini to the stand mixer and mix on medium speed until thoroughly incorporated.

5. Taste, and season with more salt if necessary.

6. Garnish with more olive oil just before serving.

[FAT PASHA]

RAPINI TABBOULEH:

1/4	cup rye berries, or any other wheat grain that you like
1/2 Tbsp	kosher salt
2	bunches rapini
1 pint	grape tomatoes, halved
1 Tbsp	chili garlic jazz (page 252)
1/2 cup	olive oil
	Lemon wedges or grilled lemon halves, for serving

1. Put the rye berries in a small pot on medium heat. Using a wooden spoon, stir until they get a bit toasty and nutty-smelling.

2. Add 3 cups water and the kosher salt to the pot and bring up to a simmer. The rye berries should take about 1 1/2 hours to cook. Once they're softer and chewy, remove the pot from the heat and allow them to cool in the liquid. If they do get a bit overcooked, strain the grains from the liquid before cooling and spread them out on a baking sheet.

3. Blanch your rapini in heavily salted water for about 30 seconds, then plunge in an ice-water bath to cool. Once they're cool, squeeze out all of the liquid from the rapini leaves with your hands, then chop the rapini into 1/2-inch pieces.

4. Drain the rye berries and place in a large bowl. Add the rapini, tomatoes, chili garlic jazz, and olive oil and mix to combine. You can add extra salt to taste, and serve with lemon wedges or grilled lemon.

MUHAMMARA:

6	roasted red bell peppers, peeled and seeded, or well-drained canned peppers will do
2 tsp	fresh lemon juice
2 tsp	pomegranate molasses
1 tsp	ground cumin
3 tsp	Aleppo pepper or hot paprika
2 tsp	finely minced garlic
2 Tbsp	olive oil
2 tsp	kosher salt
1/4 cup	pita breadcrumbs (other breadcrumbs will work as well)
1/4 cup	ground walnuts

1. Roughly chop the roasted peppers and place them in a food processor with the lemon juice, pomegranate molasses, cumin, Aleppo pepper, garlic, olive oil, and salt. Process until they have the same consistency as a relish.

2. Fold in the breadcrumbs and walnuts, and let them sit for a few hours before serving so that they can rehydrate. Add additional seasoning if necessary.

GARLIC FRIED TOMATOES:
2 pints	grape tomatoes
1/2 cup	olive oil
2 cloves	garlic
1/2 tsp	chili flakes, or more to taste
1 tsp	kosher salt
1/2 bunch	fresh parsley, chopped, for garnish

1. Preheat the oven to 425°F. Set a large oven-safe pan on medium-high heat.

2. Place the tomatoes, olive oil, and garlic in your pan and move them around to get the tomatoes well coated.

3. Season with the chili flakes and salt, and gently move the tomatoes around to coat.

4. Transfer the pan to the oven and bake for 6 to 8 minutes.

5. Remove the tomatoes from the oven and cool in the pan for a few minutes before serving.

6. Garnish with a generous helping of chopped parsley. This recipe will produce a fair bit of tomatoes, but you can use any extras for the burnt eggplant dip (page 69).

GARLIC LABNEH:
1 cup	labneh or pressed plain Greek yogurt
1 Tbsp	finely minced garlic
	Za'atar, for garnish
	Olive oil, for garnish

1. Mix the labneh and garlic together. Now it's ready!

2. Garnish with as much za'atar and olive oil as you like. We use lots.

TAHINI DIP:

1 cup	tahini
3 Tbsp	fresh lemon juice
2 tsp	olive oil, plus extra for garnish
1 tsp	kosher salt
1 tsp	finely minced garlic (as fine as you can get it)

EVERYTHING BAGEL SPICE:

1 Tbsp	dehydrated onion
1 Tbsp	dehydrated garlic
1 Tbsp	poppy seeds
1 Tbsp	black sesame seeds
1 Tbsp	white sesame seeds
1 tsp	kosher salt

1. In a food processor, combine the tahini, lemon juice, olive oil, salt, and garlic with 1 cup water. Blend until it thickens and becomes very white—it should look like a thick Greek yogurt.

2. In a large nonstick frying pan over medium-low heat, toast the dehydrated onion, dehydrated garlic, poppy seeds, black and white sesame seeds, and salt. Keep an eye on it so you don't burn anything—it should take only 1 to 2 minutes.

3. Transfer the tahini to a serving bowl and garnish with a generous amount of the everything bagel spice and plenty of olive oil.

FAT PASHA HUMMUS

ONE OF MY FIRST-EVER CULINARY CREATIONS was grilled shrimp with hummus, stuffed in a pita. I know, pure genius, right? My friend Anthony (another Anthony, obviously) was the first of my gang to get his driver's license, and we were set free. We'd drive up to the cottage for weekends of debauchery, and I'd make my classic shrimp and hummus pitas. The meal was designed in the pure spirit of road trips and freedom and friendships and no parents and many substances. Blessed be the hummus, the recipe for which evolved over time. The recipe below is loosely based on one by Yotam Ottolenghi, of course. Thank you so much, YO.

2 1/2 cups	dried chickpeas (see note)
1 tsp	baking soda
1/2 Tbsp + 1 tsp	kosher salt, divided
1 Tbsp	minced garlic
1/2 cup	tahini
7 Tbsp	fresh lemon juice
1/4 cup	olive oil
6 Tbsp	ice water

1. Soak your chickpeas overnight in 2 quarts water.

2. The next day, drain your chickpeas. Place the drained chickpeas and baking soda in a dry pot on medium heat. Stir constantly until all the excess moisture has dried up in the bottom of the pot. This will help release the skins from the chickpeas.

3. Add 6 cups water and 1/2 Tbsp salt to the pot.

4. Bring the chickpeas up to a simmer, stirring often. As the skins rise to the top of the water, skim them off with a slotted spoon and discard. Also skim off and discard the foam that rises.

5. Cook the chickpeas for 45 to 60 minutes. They'll look broken down and overcooked when they're ready. Strain the chickpeas, then return them to the pot to keep them as warm as possible.

6. In small batches, transfer the chickpeas to a food processor along with the minced garlic, and blend for a few minutes. Once the chickpeas have become a paste, add more to the processor. Never fill the food processor more than one-quarter full, and scrape down the sides if necessary. If your processor is on the smaller side, transfer the chickpea paste into a large bowl as needed, then transfer all the paste back to the processor before you add the remaining ingredients.

7. Once all the chickpeas have become a smooth paste, add the tahini, lemon juice, olive oil, 6 Tbsp ice water, and remaining 1 tsp salt.

8. Blend again until it all comes together, another 1 to 2 minutes.

9. Add any additional salt if needed, and let cool. This is best served fresh and slightly warm.

10. We garnish our hummus with braised chickpeas, chipotle powder, lemon vinaigrette, and lots of chopped parsley. You can garnish this with anything your heart desires: foie gras, merguez sausage, chopped Israeli salad, or anything else you can dream up!

[FAT PASHA]

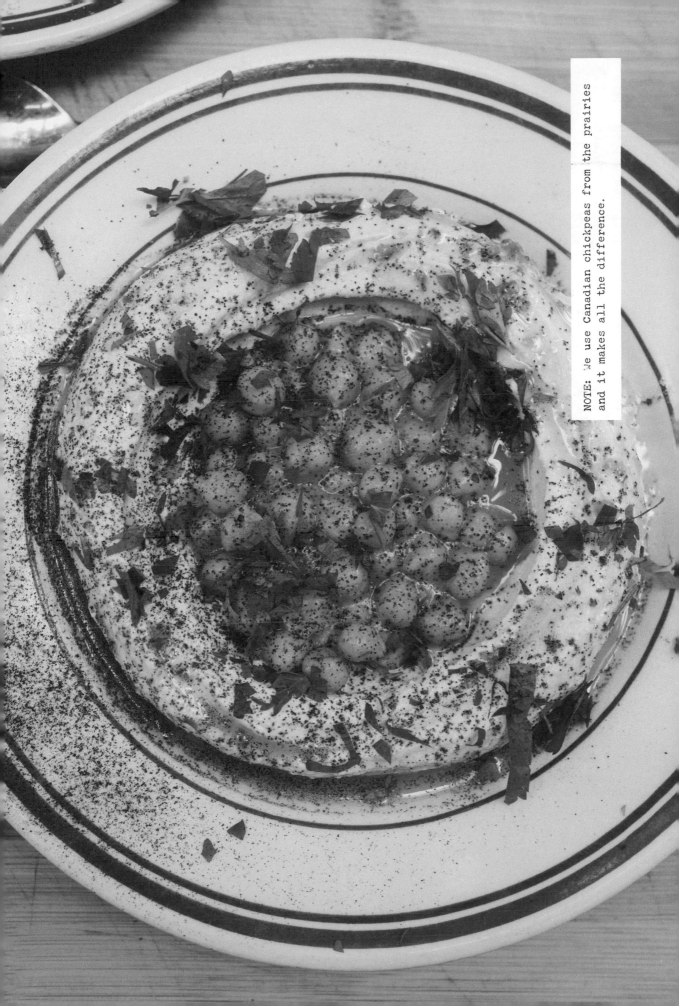

CHOPPED LIVER

IN MY WORLD, I have a handful of "Very Important Restaurants," which on any given day could include but would not be limited to the following: Zuni Café, Chez Panisse, Grand Central Oyster Bar, House of Chan, Mario's Bohemian Cigar Store, Katz's Delicatessen, Russ and Daughters, Bistrot Paul Bert, Le Severo, Huitrerie Régis, Swiss Chalet, Pancer's Original Delicatessen, and Sammy's Roumanian Steakhouse.

Anyways, where was I? This is a very important dish from the very important restaurant Sammy's Roumanian. Their chopped liver with grilled sweetbreads and vodka on ice is one of the greatest happy meals of all time. I took my business partner, Rob, there once for his virgin food tour. We ate liver and sweetbreads with vodka on ice for lunch and he didn't complain about the broken sewer smell even once.

GRIBENES:

1/2 lb	chicken skins
	Kosher salt
1 lb	chicken livers, rinsed well and dried
1 Tbsp	duck salt (page 250)
1/2 cup	canola oil
2 Tbsp	arak, divided
3 Tbsp	caramelized onions (page 17)
3 Tbsp	grated radish
1/4 cup	schmaltz or duck fat, melted, + extra for garnish
2	large hard-boiled eggs, sliced
4 pieces	grilled challah (page 65 or store-bought), for serving

1. Preheat the oven to 350°F.

2. First, you'll prepare the gribenes, or chicken skins, which will go on top of your liver as a garnish. Place your chicken skins in a pot of salted water and simmer for about 30 minutes. Strain, reserving the liquid. Transfer the liquid to a bowl and cool in the fridge. After it's cold, you can remove and save the schmaltz that will have hardened on top of the poaching water. Place the schmaltz in a separate bowl, and discard the poaching liquid.

3. While the liquid cools, dry the poached chicken skins with a clean dish towel. Once the chicken skins are dry, transfer to a baking sheet and bake for 20 to 25 minutes, until golden and crispy. Remove the chicken skins from the oven and season with salt. Set aside.

4. While your chicken skins are in the oven, season your rinsed chicken livers with the duck salt and let sit for 1 hour.

5. Heat a large pan on high and add the canola oil. Sear the chicken livers on both sides until they're caramelized, about 1 to 2 minutes per side. Do not overcrowd your pan! You may need to do this in batches.

6. Once your chicken livers are seared, deglaze the pan with 1 Tbsp of the arak. Use a wooden spoon to scrape up any brown bits on the bottom of your pan—they're delicious.

7. Put the seared chicken livers and the remaining arak in a food processor.

8. Blend the livers and, while the machine is running, add 4 Tbsp water and 1/4 cup of the schmaltz (see note). Process until smooth.

9. Cool the pâté and serve in a bowl with the caramelized onions, grated radish, hard-boiled eggs, and gribenes. Dress with extra melted schmaltz and mix tableside. Serve with some grilled challah or your preference of bread.

NOTE: You can also use duck fat in place of the schmaltz.

[FAT PASHA]

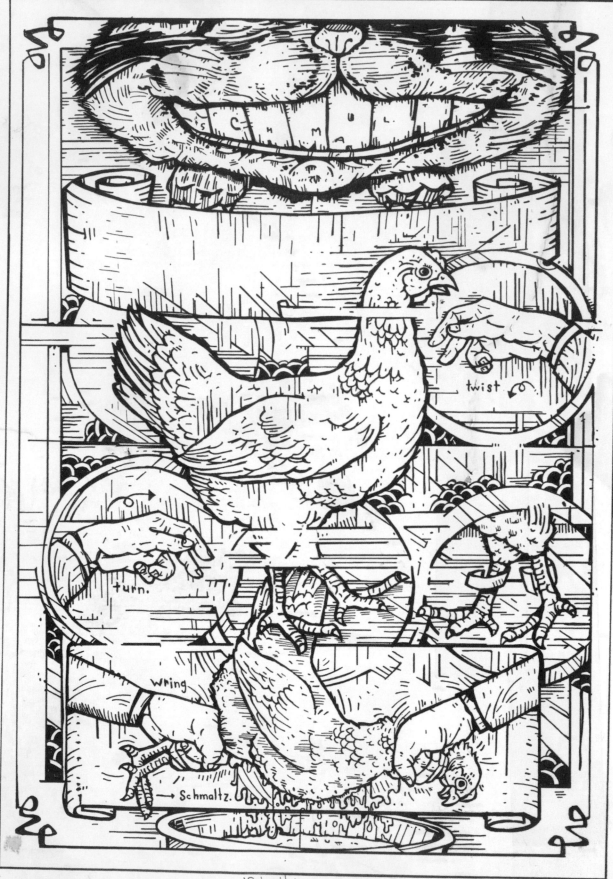

'Schmaltz'

GRILLED PASHA CHICKEN

EVERY CHICKEN DISH I'VE EVER COOKED and every chicken dish I've ever shown or taught anybody else to cook, I learned at Jonathan Waxman's now gone but never forgotten restaurant, Washington Park, in New York. The actual recipe was taught to me by Chef Lynn McNeely on that proud day when I was deemed ready for the grill. Cooking the bird skin side down on medium-high heat to start gives it a dreamy, crispy skin that shatters in your mouth. Finishing flesh side down ensures perfection every time.

CHICKEN:
4	boneless half chickens (see note)
3 Tbsp	dried Greek oregano
3 Tbsp	dried mint
	Kosher salt and freshly ground black pepper
2 tsp	canola oil

TZATZIKI:
1	English cucumber
1 tsp	kosher salt
1 1/2 cups	labneh or pressed plain Greek yogurt
2 tsp	chili garlic jazz (page 252)
2 tsp	fresh lemon juice

TOMATO SALAD:
4	large heirloom tomatoes, different colors and varieties
1/4 cup	olive oil
4 Tbsp	chopped fresh mint
	Kosher salt and freshly ground black pepper

1. Place your chickens in a dish and toss with the oregano, mint, salt, and pepper. Let marinate in the fridge for 30 minutes or overnight.

2. For the tzatziki, use a large box grater to grate the cucumber, then transfer to a fine-mesh strainer set over a bowl and mix with the salt. Let this sit overnight in the fridge as well—you want to make sure that all of the moisture has drained from the cucumbers, so it's important to give them time. The next day, transfer the cucumbers to a clean dish towel and squeeze out any remaining water. Try to remove as much water as you can. Discard any liquid remaining in the bowl, then return the cucumbers to the bowl. Add the labneh, chili garlic jazz, and lemon juice. Taste for seasoning, and add more salt if needed.

3. Preheat your barbecue to medium heat and brush the grill bars with oil. Grill the chickens skin side down. If the skins are sticking, leave them alone; they'll release when they're ready! Once the chicken is about three-quarters of the way cooked, about 12 minutes, flip it over and finish on the other side for 4 to 6 minutes. You can check to see if it's done using a meat thermometer—if the chicken reaches 165°F, it's ready.

4. For the tomato salad, right before serving, cut your tomatoes into wedges and toss with the olive oil, mint, salt, and pepper. Serve this all together on a platter, the messier the better!

NOTE: You can ask your butcher to debone a half chicken for you, but if they can't, just get four boneless breasts and four boneless thighs, both with skin.

[FAT PASHA]

GRILLED SALMON WITH RAMP RELISH

WILD LEEKS (RAMPS) ARE GOD'S GIFT TO ME, my cottage, and my belly. I am no hunter and certainly not a regular forager, but I can still spot a wild leek from quite a distance. I go foraging once a year, in spring and only in spring, and only for ramps. I take some sort of implement for digging from my mom's kitchen drawer, grab my beautiful son, Simon, and off we go to stuff a shopping bag full. Michael and Nobuyo Stadtländer, of Eigensinn Farm, throw a festival dedicated to this incredible ingredient each spring, in the back forest wonderland of their property. Sometimes it's raining, sometimes it's snowing, sometimes it's hot, and sometimes it's cold, but it's always as much fun as you could possibly have. My partner, Rob, has a farm one county road over from Eigensinn Farm, but he doesn't actually farm anything. For an area that's ridiculously rich with wild leeks, Rob has none. He can't even farm god's gift.

RAMP RELISH:

1/2 lb	cleaned ramps
1/2 bunch	fresh parsley, chopped
1/2 bunch	fresh cilantro, chopped
2 tsp	honey
2 1/2 Tbsp	baco noir vinegar or any other red wine vinegar
3 Tbsp	olive oil
	Kosher salt and freshly ground black pepper to taste
2 (10 oz)	fillets chinook or Atlantic salmon
	Kosher salt and freshly ground black pepper
2 tsp	canola oil

1. For the ramp relish, preheat your barbecue on high. Grill the ramps until tender with a bit of char, about 2 minutes. Remove them from the grill and roughly chop them. Transfer to a large bowl and mix with the chopped parsley and cilantro, honey, vinegar, olive oil, salt, and pepper. Set aside and serve at room temperature.

2. Season your fish with salt and pepper and allow to sit at room temperature for 20 minutes.

3. Get your barbecue as hot as possible. Scrape the grill bars extra-clean and oil them with a towel or with oil spray to help the fish not stick. Rub your salmon fillets with 1 tsp canola oil each, but don't use too much or you'll get a lot of flare-up from the grill.

4. Turn down the barbecue to medium-high heat and cook the salmon for 3 to 4 minutes per side for medium-rare. If you like your fish a bit more well done, add 1 or 2 minutes per side.

5. Cut each fillet in half, and serve the fish with the ramp relish on top.

GRILLED ASPARAGUS WITH TOUM

EVEN MORE THAN WILD LEEKS, the Passover meal is really the first harbinger of spring for me. It marks the first time in the year that we get to actually use green vegetables. After a cold, hard winter, there is always so much to look forward to—asparagus and sweet peas, especially. Both are easy to use, local, and delicious, and they're always served at my Passover celebrations. The garlicky-sweet toum dressing here is super-interesting and a very cool garnish for these new vegetables.

TOUM:

1 head	garlic, peeled
1 1/2 tsp	honey
1 Tbsp	kosher salt
	Juice of 1 lemon
1 cup	canola oil
2 lb	asparagus

1. In a blender, puree the garlic with 3 Tbsp water.

2. Add the honey, salt, and lemon juice to the blender, turn it back on, and process until well blended.

3. With the blender on low, slowly add the canola oil to emulsify. Keep the lid on, and add the oil through the opening of the lid so the mixture doesn't splatter. The mixture should be thick and creamy when done.

4. Bring a large pot of salted water to a boil, prepare an ice bath and preheat your barbecue on high heat. When the water is boiling, blanch the asparagus for 30 seconds, then transfer immediately to the ice bath. Finish by charring the asparagus on the barbecue, about 2 minutes per side. Serve with the toum drizzled overtop or on the side.

[FAT PASHA]

NOTE: Jeremy and Mike, the chefs at Fat Pasha, first introduced me to toum. They also like to serve this with a sprinkling of hazelnut dukkah, which is an Egyptian condiment.

BUTTERED SWEET PEA RICE

MY OLDER SISTER, RANDI ROSE, is a cardiologist. My younger brother, Lorne Rose, is a lawyer. Both underachieving siblings. When we were kids and my folks would go out for the night, Randi's go-to dish was rice with enough butter to choke a cow. A bowl of steaming rice that you slowly mix with cold butter is divine. Randi is a cardiologist, did I mention that?

1/2 Tbsp	kosher salt
1 1/2 cups	basmati rice
4 Tbsp	slivered almonds
1 Tbsp	chili garlic jazz (page 252)
1/4 cup	butter
2 tsp	kosher salt
1 cup	shelled sweet peas
1 cup	sugar snap peas, sliced in 1/2-inch pieces
2 cups	pea shoots or snow pea greens + extra for garnish

1. Preheat the oven to 375°F. Bring 2 cups water and the salt to a boil in a small oven-safe pot. As soon as the water comes to a boil, stir in the rice, cover with a lid, and put in the oven for 20 minutes. Once it's done, spread the rice out onto a tray to cool. This is a great way to cook rice for most dishes.

2. While the rice cooks, toast the slivered almonds in a nonstick pan over medium-low heat. Stir constantly for about 2 to 3 minutes or until the almonds are just starting to brown. Keep an eye on them so they don't burn, and as soon as they're done, transfer them to a bowl.

3. Once the rice is done and cooled, heat a large pan on medium-high. When the pan is hot, place 1/2 cup water and the chili garlic jazz, butter, and salt in the pan. Turn the heat up to high and let the liquid come up to a boil.

4. Add the cooked rice to the pan and let it cook until hot. Add your sweet and snap peas, mix to combine, and cook for another 30 seconds.

5. Once the rice mixture has come together and tastes delicious, add the pea shoots at the very last second and toss quickly before plating.

6. Top with the toasted almonds and the extra pea shoots.

[FAT PASHA]

The Cauliflower

Whole roasted cauliflower is to Anthony Rose what "Don't Worry Be Happy" is to Bobby McFerrin—only one component of a long and diverse career, but the one he'll always be most closely associated with, for better or for worse.

"I'm not a huge fan of the dish myself," Anthony admits. "I find it a little messy and a little confusing. I mean, there's a lot going on there; it's just stacking bills on bills on bills."

Toronto went crazy for it, though. The radio and newspapers sent reporters to talk to Anthony about it. Video crews showed up to film it being made and, for a while, it was practically law that anyone who ate it had to post it on Instagram first.

When the great cauliflower shortage of 2016 hit (a problem that Anthony fears he might have had a hand in exacerbating), the dish only became more popular. "It was so expensive, we started listing it on the menu as 'market price,'" Anthony says. "Have you ever seen 'market price' for a vegetable on a menu? It's crazy. At one point we were charging $38 for a cauliflower and people would still line up for it. It was nuts. We were thinking about taking it off the menu, but we couldn't. Honestly, though, it's nice to have a dish like that in your repertoire. As a chef, you're lucky to have a dish like that on any menu."

WHOLE ROASTED CAULIFLOWER

SERVES 2 TO 4

WHAT EYAL SHANI HAS DONE WITH FOOD in Israel is outstanding. One of my favorite dining experiences was at Ha'Salon restaurant in Tel Aviv on Purim a few years ago, with staff and guests dressed in costumes and dancing on the bar. I've eaten Eyal's whole roasted cauliflower in Israel and at his restaurant Miznon in Paris. This recipe is an homage to him. His is simple and delicious; mine is dressed to the nines and messy. Both are wicked, and I blame him for the Great Cauliflower Catastrophe of 2016.

1	gorgeous head cauliflower
1/4 cup	olive oil
	Kosher salt and freshly ground black pepper
6 Tbsp	tahini, thinned with a little extra water if necessary
4 Tbsp	shredded halloumi
4 Tbsp	toasted Pakistani pine nuts or another variety if needed
4 Tbsp	pomegranate seeds

SKHUG:

1 bunch	fresh cilantro
1 bunch	fresh parsley
1	bird's eye chili or red finger chili
2 Tbsp	minced garlic
1 Tbsp	kosher salt
4	ice cubes
2 Tbsp	olive oil

1. Preheat the oven to 425°F. Bring a large pot of salted water to a boil—the pot should be big enough to fit the whole cauliflower. Clean any excess greens from your cauliflower.

2. Drop the cauliflower into the boiling water, floret side down, and let poach for 2 to 3 minutes.

3. Remove from the water and let sit on a baking sheet for 5 minutes so the steam can escape and the cauliflower can dry out a bit. Leave the cauliflower on the baking sheet, and score an X into the top of it about 2 inches deep.

4. Once the cauliflower has stopped steaming, drench it in olive oil and season with salt and pepper. Roast it on the baking sheet in the oven for 20 minutes or so, until you get some caramelization on the outside. Don't be afraid of some good char; it's delicious!

5. While the cauliflower roasts, make the skhug. Combine the cilantro, parsley, chili, garlic, salt, ice and olive oil in a blender. Blend until it becomes a paste.

6. To serve, put your cauliflower on a plate and garnish with the tahini first, then the skhug, followed by the halloumi and finishing with the pine nuts and pomegranate seeds. Stab with a steak knife and serve whole.

[FAT PASHA]

"The Great Cauliflower Catastrophe of 2016"

THE CHOUX IS JUST

Gucci.

SUFGANIYOT

THIS RECIPE COMES FROM THE LAZY COOK who lives inside of me. Still, it turned out to be awesome. Bonnie Stern gave me the idea to use the choux pastry instead of the classic doughnut dough, and it is just Gucci man. It's bigger and fluffier, and there's so much more room inside to stuff with goodness.

CHOUX PASTRY:

2/3 cup	unsalted butter
3 1/3 cups	all-purpose flour
1/2 tsp	kosher salt
1 1/2 Tbsp	white sugar
10	large eggs

CHOCOLATE CUSTARD:

2	egg yolks
2 Tbsp	white sugar, divided
1 cup	heavy cream (35%), divided
1/2 tsp	vanilla paste or extract
1/4 cup	70% chocolate (or any dark chocolate will do)

CINNAMON SUGAR:

1 tsp	ground cinnamon
1/2 cup	icing sugar
	Vegetable oil, for deep frying
	Whipped cream, for garnish (optional)

1. For the choux pastry, place the butter in a large pot with 2 cups water. Bring to a bubble. Then, over medium heat, add the flour, salt, and sugar and start vigorously stirring with a wooden spoon until your choux is cooked. This should take about 7 to 10 minutes and a lot of determination. Once your choux is cooked, transfer it to a stand mixer with the paddle attachment. Turn on medium-low speed and add the eggs one at a time while the dough is still hot. Make sure each egg is fully incorporated before adding the next one. Once the mix is ready, cover with plastic wrap and refrigerate until fully cold, about 1 hour.

2. For the chocolate custard, in a small pot over low heat, combine the egg yolks, 1 Tbsp sugar, 1/2 cup heavy cream, and the vanilla. Whisk constantly until the mixture starts to thicken. At the same time, melt your chocolate in a double boiler until liquid (see page 207), or microwave it in 30-second increments until melted. Mix the melted chocolate and custard, then set aside to fully cool. With a hand mixer, whip the remaining 1 Tbsp sugar and 1/2 cup cream to stiff peaks, then fold the whipped cream into the chocolate custard.

3. Mix your cinnamon and icing sugar together in a small bowl to garnish your sufganiyot!

4. To fry your sufganiyot, heat a deep fryer or large pot of oil to 325°F. A kitchen thermometer is very helpful here, and make sure to use enough oil so that the sufganiyot can move around freely. In small batches, drop in a heaping tablespoon of choux paste into the oil, being careful not to let it splatter. Cook for 3 to 4 minutes per side until the sufganiyot have tripled in size and are hollow and light. You can tell they're cooked if they maintain their shape when removed from the oil. If they aren't cooked enough, they'll collapse. Once the sufganiyot have had about 15 seconds to rest and there is no visible oil left on the surface, dust with cinnamon sugar. Start on the next batch of sufganiyot, making sure to let the oil come back up to temperature between batches. Continue until you've used all your choux pastry.

5. You can plate these any way you like: stuff the sufganiyot with the custard using a piping bag, or spread the custard out on a plate and place the sufganiyot overtop. Garnish with whipped cream if using.

NOTE: I love Jell-O pudding, and please do not be too much of a snob to agree with me. It is perfect alongside this dish and so many others.

[FAT PASHA]

L'Chaim!

MANISCHEWITZ VERMOUTH

SERVES A LOT

I FIND THAT NO ONE REALLY LIKES MANISCHEWITZ, except for the kids who drink it as their first taste of alcohol. But when we opened Fat Pasha, I wanted to use it for something funky and different and cool and Jew-y. This is it. We also make jelly out of this stuff.

	Zest of 1/2 lemon
	Zest of 1/2 orange
1 bottle	Manischewitz kosher wine
5	whole cloves
5	juniper berries
1	star anise
1 tsp	ground sumac
1 tsp	black peppercorns
3 oz	brandy (we use St-Rémy)
1	small piece gentian root (about 1/2 tsp, see note)
1	small piece wormwood (about 1/2 tsp, see note)

1. In a large container, combine the lemon and orange zests, Manischewitz wine, cloves, juniper berries, star anise, sumac, peppercorns, and brandy. Refrigerate for 3 days.

2. Add the gentian root and wormwood to the mixture and refrigerate for 1 more day.

3. Strain the mixture and pour it into a wooden barrel or a mason jar. Let this age for at least 2 weeks.

4. Serve as an after-dinner digestif or a nightcap!

[FAT PASHA]

NOTE: You can find gentian root and wormwood at health food stores.

NO ONE REALLY LIKES MANISCHEWITZ... WE MAKE *jelly* OUT OF THE STUFF.

SCHMALTZ APPETIZING
PURVEYORS OF FINE FISH

The great Bagel Debate- NY, MTL, Toronto

ROWS OF COLORFUL SELTZER STUBBIES IN OLD-SCHOOL FLAVORS—raspberry
soda, lemon lime, celery—are lined up on shelves inside the brand-spanking-new
Schmaltz Appetizing. The human lineup, a crowd of hungry, hungry hipsters
looking for dishes their bubbes and zaidys would have loved—bagels with a
smear of scallion cream cheese, lemon dill gravlax, Nova lox, a nice egg
salad—snakes out the door.

Schmaltz is an appetizing store—two appetizing stores, actually, now that this
larger, Ossington Avenue shop has opened to supplement the original location,
a rustic little beach shack behind Fat Pasha. An appetizing store, of course,
sells everything to do with bagels. That is to say, it sells bagels, but
doesn't make them; that's a bagel shop. And it's not a deli, because a deli is
where you get your pickles and stuff. These are fine distinctions, but
important ones. Before Anthony came along, appetizing stores in Toronto were
also nearly extinct.

"They used to be everywhere in Toronto," he says, "all up and down Spadina,
but the last one just closed a couple of years ago."

There are still plenty of bagel shops and delis and plain old kosher
restaurants in the city, and elements of the best of them are woven into the
DNA of Schmaltz.

"I wanted Schmaltz to be like those places I went to all the time growing up,"
Anthony says. "You go to somewhere like Bagel World on Wilson today and it's
the same as it was 30 years ago, probably more if you're old enough. You'll
bump into five or six people you know if you're a Toronto Jew. The servers
will get mad at you if you order wrong. It's nostalgic and it's fun. It's not
great, but it's perfect.

"United Bakers is incredible too. You go there for lunch and it's just packed.
Their menu is huge and they've got everything, but I've been going there
forever and I only ever get three things: pea soup, lox with eggs and onions,
and the whitefish platter.

"And then you've got Gryfe's. Now, Gryfe's is great, and highly specific to
Toronto. It's one of those local institutions that's been owned by the same
family for 50 or 60 years. When I was a kid, my grandfather, Simon Gottlieb,
would go to Gryfe's at six in the morning and get these steaming hot bagels
and drop them off at all his children's homes. As a memory, Gryfe's looms so
large in my mind. At Schmaltz, we carry their pizza bagels [not really a
bagel] and their blueberry buns [a typical Toronto Jewish dessert item]."

The personal connection and importance of the old Jewish places meant that Anthony wanted to source all of the ingredients for Schmaltz very carefully. The bags of potato chips come (in flavors such as sea salt, jalapeño, and ketchup) from Covered Bridge in New Brunswick, the crackers are from Evelyn's, the matzoh is from Streit's. Schmaltz makes only a few things in-house. The gefilte fish, latkes, and three different types of cured salmon are all homemade, but almost everything else comes from people who specialize in doing one thing, or just a handful of things, extremely well.

"We don't smoke our own fish at Schmaltz because there's people doing wicked smoked fish in Ontario and around," Anthony explains. "Wolfhead is the best, though. They're from Jail Island, New Brunswick. The father originally started this fish farm called Jail Island, and it was touted as being the first environmentally sound fish farm. All they do is smoked salmon. They got famous when the Queen said it was her favorite smoked salmon ever, and it is excellent. Soon it will be Meghan Markle's favorite as well.

"I'm also obsessed with Purdy's Fish Market's Lake Erie whitefish. I've been using their stuff for years. They specialize in fresh-caught lake fish: pickerel, perch, and whitefish. But I would say that 90 percent of their catch goes to New York State, because it's got the largest Jewish population. Their two biggest clients are the Jews and the Asian population."

Among the biggest decisions before opening Schmaltz was to determine what kind of bagel to use. Anthony agonized over it, knowing that the type of bagel was going to be the single most controversial part of the whole experiment. "There's so much bullshit with bagels," he says. "Everyone's an expert, and you're just guaranteed to get a lot of people mad at you. When people talk bagels, it's not a debate, man, it's a fucking war. It's like opening a barbecue place."

When you order a bagel at Schmaltz, you get a Kiva's bagel. It's a great bagel and this keeps most people happy, but as with all things bagel, it's not a perfect situation. "We experimented with bagels from a few locations at first," Anthony admits. "But we ran into problems with delivery schedules or price raising. We did serve Montreal bagels for a little while. I love Montreal bagels. They're dark and dense, and there's not a lot of salt in them. To me, a Montreal bagel coming out of the toaster with butter on it is the greatest thing in the world. But I was there the first day we brought in Montreal bagels, and it was nuts. You offer a Montreal bagel and suddenly there's a huge argument. 'Oh, why do you have this type of bagel and not a New York bagel? Why do you serve it this way?' We did Montreal bagels for one weekend and called it quits. Ultimately, Kiva's seemed like a good compromise."

There's a secret plot behind Schmaltz, though. It's one that stays hidden behind the more dramatic bagel wars, and it's one that Anthony's never told anyone before now.

"Honestly," he says, "I think my main goal with Schmaltz is to bring back the herring. I fucking love herring. No one eats it except me and the old buggers, but we're going to try to get it back out there. Hopefully, with a larger, younger audience, we'll be able to do that."

EGG SALAD

I CAN NEVER, ever eat egg salad made by anyone other than my mom, Linda. Mostly,
I like it piled on Bonnie Stern's toasted and generously buttered challah (page 65)
and topped with a bit of salt, and nothing else. Linda grates her eggs with the
finest side of a box grater for the finest egg salad.

12	large eggs
4 Tbsp	finely chopped scallions
2 Tbsp	chopped fresh dill
3/4 cup	mayo
2 dashes	Tabasco
1 tsp	fresh lemon juice
1 tsp	kosher salt
1/2 tsp	freshly ground black pepper
	Toasted challah (page 65 or store-bought), for serving

1. Bring a large pot of salted water to a boil. With a slotted spoon, drop your eggs into the boiling water and let boil for 11 minutes. Transfer the eggs to a bowl of ice water for another 11 minutes, then peel immediately.

2. Grate your eggs on the finest side of a box grater, or chop your eggs to your desired texture and place in a bowl.

3. Add the scallions, dill, mayo, Tabasco, lemon juice, salt, and pepper to the bowl, and mix. Serve with toasted challah.

[SCHMALTZ APPETIZING]

WHITEFISH SALAD

THE SUPER HEEBSTER SANDWICH at Russ and Daughters in New York is quite possibly my favorite sandwich of all time. I lived around the corner from the shop when I was a young cook in the 90s, and it was on my list of tourist attractions that everyone had to visit. Most of the whitefish in North America comes from the Great Lakes in Canada, and most of it goes to satisfy the Jewish demand for this delicacy, which is massive.

1 (2 lb)	whole smoked whitefish, cleaned and gutted (most good Jewish groceries will have this fish)
1/2 cup	mayo
1	Tbsp labneh or pressed plain Greek yogurt
1 tsp	kosher salt
2 tsp	fresh lemon juice
6	poppy seed bagels, heavily toasted and buttered

1. To remove the flesh from your whitefish, start by removing the skin, the fin, and the head. Remove all the large bones. Pick the meat away from the smaller bones and the skin, and go slowly as you do it. You need to remove all the pin bones, though a little bit of skin won't kill you. Start flaking the fish apart slowly.

2. Once you have removed all the bones, you have to do this again. Go through the meat at least two more times closely and look for more bones. These bones can be tricky.

3. Mix the whitefish with the mayo, labneh, salt, and lemon juice. Serve with the toasted and buttered bagels, and you're ready to go.

[SCHMALTZ APPETIZING]

SERVES 6
or
1 HUNGRY KID

NOTE: Make a sandwich with your gefilte fish—it's not just for the holidays.

GEFILTE FISH

WE MAKE AND SELL THIS BEAUTY during the High Holidays: Rosh Hashanah and Yom Kippur. I like the addition of smoked whitefish here for texture and flavor. You need to answer an important question before you make this recipe, though. Are you a sweet or salt-and-pepper gefilte fish kind of person? The correct answer is salt and pepper. Every. Single. Time.

POACHING LIQUID:

2 tsp	fennel seeds
2 tsp	coriander seeds
1	small onion, roughly chopped
1	stalk celery, roughly chopped
2	bay leaves
1	star anise
4 tsp	kosher salt
1 lb	whitefish fillet, skin and bones removed
4 Tbsp	canola oil
1	small white onion, diced small
1	medium carrot, peeled and diced small
1 tsp	ground turmeric
1/4 tsp	chili flakes
2	large eggs
6 Tbsp	matzoh meal or panko
1 tsp	kosher salt
1 Tbsp	sugar

1. Prepare your poaching liquid. In a large pot, combine the fennel seeds, coriander seeds, onions, celery, bay leaves, star anise, and salt with 2 quarts water. Set the pot over medium heat for 15 minutes so the flavors can incorporate. Once done, strain out and discard the solids and keep the liquid for poaching the fish.

2. Cube your fish and put it in the freezer for 20 minutes while you get everything else ready.

3. In a medium pan over medium-low heat, heat the canola oil and sauté the onions, carrots, turmeric, and chili flakes. Just sweat out the vegetables, but don't let them start to color. Remove the pan from the heat and set aside to cool.

4. Mix your cooled veg and firmed fish cubes together and put through a grinder. If you do not have a grinder, you can do this in a food processor, but be careful not to overheat the fish. If the fish starts to heat up, put the mixture back in the freezer to cool down for a few minutes, then keep going. Your finished consistency should be sausage-like. Once the fish and veg are ground, transfer the mixture to a large bowl and combine it with the eggs, matzoh meal, salt, and sugar. At this point, let the mixture sit overnight so that the matzoh meal absorbs all the moisture.

5. To cook the gefilte fish, set your strained poaching liquid back on the stove and bring to a simmer over medium heat. You can roll the fish in plastic wrap to make "sausages," or you can shape tablespoonfuls to make more of a meatball.

6. Drop your gefilte fish sausages or balls into the simmering poaching liquid. Depending on the size, they can take between 5 and 10 minutes to cook. They're done when they've reached an internal temperature of 160°F.

HERRING AND ONIONS TWO WAYS

HERRING HAS BEEN A LOST DELICACY FOR SO LONG, and I'm so sorry, herring, because I love you so much. I'm bringing back these salty, fatty, and adorable fishies, but I need help. Please sign the petition below, as these darlings seem to have skipped about two generations of Jews and gentiles alike.

8 oz	your herring of choice (schmaltz, matjes, or smoked)
1/2 cup	very thinly sliced Spanish onions
4 Tbsp	Kozlik's Triple Crunch mustard or another grainy mustard
OR	
4 Tbsp	sour cream
2 Tbsp	chopped fresh dill
4 Tbsp	thinly sliced scallions
	Dark rye bread or bagels, toasted and buttered, for serving

1. Chances are that your herring will come soaked in brine or oil. You'll need to completely drain your fillets and dry them before you cut them, unless, of course, you're eating whole fillets, which is awesome!

2. Take your dried fillets and cut them widthwise into 1-inch chunks.

3. Mix the herring chunks with the onions and mustard OR the sour cream, dill, and scallions.

4. Serve with a nice dark rye bread or bagels that have been toasted dark and heavily buttered.

Herring—Bringing it Back

LEMON DILL GRAVLAX

CURING SALMON IS SO EASY, but you need some time and patience. At a basic level, you can cure fish with salt and sugar. If you add some other ingredients like gin, lemon zest, maple syrup, or grated beetroot, then the simple salmon quickly becomes the king of the sea. Smoked salmon is cured first and then usually cold-smoked after. Wolfhead is double-smoked and from New Brunswick and is the Queen's favorite. So, if you ever meet her, as a good subject you can say that it's your favorite too.

1 (2 to 3 lb)	center-cut Atlantic salmon fillet, scaled and pin-boned
2 1/2 lb	kosher salt (I recommend Diamond Crystal)
2 1/2 lb	turbinado or brown sugar
1 bunch	fresh dill, divided
	Zest of 3 lemons, divided
1/4 cup	aquavit or vodka

1. Ask your fishmonger when their Atlantic salmon comes in and whether they can set some aside for you. You've got to start with a fresh and fatty product.

2. In a large bowl, mix the salt and sugar together thoroughly to make your cure. Spread about a quarter of the mixture evenly in a large casserole dish.

3. Lay the salmon, skin side down, onto the cure.

4. Sprinkle a small amount of the cure onto the flesh of the salmon, and gently massage it in with your hands. Then garnish generously with half of the chopped dill and the zest of 2 of the lemons.

5. Evenly sprinkle the aquavit or vodka over the salmon, then cover with the remaining cure. You need to make sure that you can't see the fish anymore! Cover the dish with plastic wrap or aluminum foil.

6. Find a nice flat place in your fridge and slide the casserole dish in. This will need to be refrigerated for 2 to 3 days, depending on how firm and salty you want your fish. Flip the salmon once daily, and make sure that it's always covered in the cure.

7. Once the fish has firmed up to a texture that you like, rinse the cure off with water and dry with paper towel. Garnish with the remaining chopped dill and the zest of the last lemon and let dry covered in the fridge for another 12 hours.

[SCHMALTZ APPETIZING]

BEETROOT GRAVLAX
1 side gravlax
3 lb red beets

1. Proceed to make gravlax as described
   on the previous page, but omit the
   dill and lemon zest.

2. Peel and roughly chop your raw
   beets, then place in a blender and
   puree. Add a little water if
   necessary to puree them.

3. Once your salmon is cured and dried,
   cover it in a thick coating of the
   beet puree and leave for 24 hours.
   Your salmon should now be super-
   bright!

Cel-Ray Soda

Dr. Brown's Cel-Ray soda (the celery-flavored soda) has been
very hard to come by in Canada these last few years. Like Skippy
peanut butter, it has mysteriously disappeared, at first slowly,
then quickly, and then altogether. I didn't know I missed it
until I started looking for it. GONE.

I tried very hard to make my own to mostly disappointing
results, so I gave up. We now import it ourselves by the
truckload along with some other choice Dr. Brown's sodas.

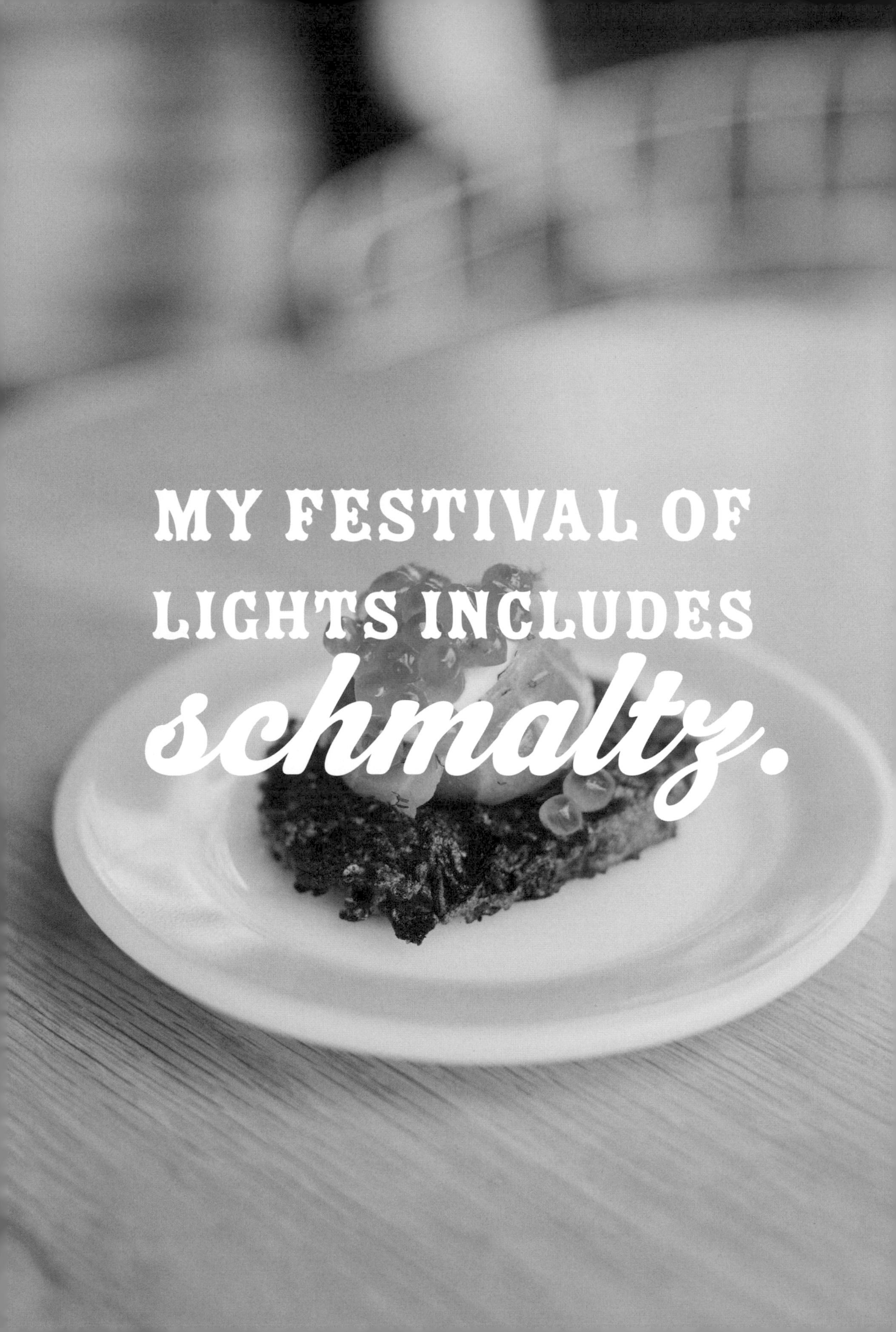

MY FESTIVAL OF
LIGHTS INCLUDES
schmaltz.

SCHMALTZ LATKES

YOU CAN FRY YOUR LATKES in oil or butter or whatever you want. My festival of lights includes schmaltz, the generously delicious rendered fat from chicken skins. Schmaltz adds flavor, depth, and overall intensity to an already scrumptious dish. You can serve this with my mom's applesauce recipe or with smoked salmon and caviar on top, which is next level.

LATKES:

1	small white onion
1 Tbsp	kosher salt, divided
1 1/3 lb	Yukon Gold potatoes
1/2 tsp	freshly ground black pepper
2/3 cup	matzoh meal or panko
2 Tbsp	all-purpose flour
1	large egg
1	large egg yolk
	Schmaltz or duck fat, for frying
1/2 cup	sour cream, for dipping

APPLESAUCE:

5 lb	Spy apples (use McIntosh if Spys aren't available)
2 sticks	cinnamon
3 Tbsp	white sugar
1/2 tsp	kosher salt
OR	
	smoked salmon, for serving
	caviar, for serving

1. First start the latkes. Peel and slice your onion very thinly, then season with 1/2 Tbsp salt and let sit for 20 to 30 minutes to get all the juices out.

2. As the onions sit, you can make the applesauce. Peel, core, and cut your apples into large chunks. Place the apples in a large pot with 1/2 cup water, the cinnamon sticks, sugar, and salt. Stir to combine, and bring to a simmer over medium heat. Cook for 20 minutes or until the apples start to break down, stirring occasionally. Once the apples are soft, remove the pot from the heat.

3. Let the apples cool, then remove and discard the cinnamon sticks. If you like, mash the apples with a potato masher for a smoother consistency. Check for seasoning and add extra cinnamon if desired. You can make this ahead and then reheat to serve over your latkes or serve at room temperature.

4. Return to the latkes. When your onions are almost ready, wash your potatoes and grate them on the fine side of a box grater, then place the potatoes and their juices in a large bowl and mix in the onions. The acid in the onion juice will stop the potatoes from oxidizing too quickly.

5. Add 1/2 Tbsp salt and the pepper, matzoh meal, flour, egg, and egg yolk, and stir to combine. Let the dough hang out for 5 minutes.

6. Weigh the latkes into 2 oz balls or use an ice-cream scoop that will make the size that you want. Firmly squeeze all of the juice out of the latkes, form back into balls, and set aside on a clean dish towel to dry a bit.

7. Gently warm your schmaltz in a large pan over medium heat. Add three to five latke balls to your pan, depending on the pan size, and fry for 1 minute. Don't overcrowd the pan!

8. Press the latkes down with a spatula and they'll naturally become more of a patty shape.

9. Let them fry until they're a beautiful golden brown, about 3 to 4 minutes per side. Remove the latkes from the fat and put aside on a plate lined with paper towel to absorb any excess fat. Season with more salt and serve with sour cream and applesauce on the side or with smoked salmon, caviar and sour cream on top.

[SCHMALTZ APPETIZING]

NOTE: If you're making these at Passover, you can omit the flour.

LOX, EGGS, AND ONIONS

"THE BAGEL"—or, as it was locally and lovingly known, "The Dirty Bagel"—was an old bagel joint and institution in Toronto. That wasn't the actual name on the sign, but the actual name if you were in the know. The place is gone now, but it once reigned supreme for that go-to, mouthwatering, early morning brunch—before brunch was even a thing. Eggs and onions on a twister bagel was the best thing at the Dirty Bagel, but if you were baller, you went with lox, eggs, and onions.

12 slices	Nova lox
2 Tbsp	unsalted butter
8	large eggs, beaten
1/2 cup	caramelized onions (page 17)
1/4 cup	crème fraîche
	Kosher salt and freshly ground black pepper
4	bagels or 4 slices challah (page 65 or store-bought)

1. Julienne the lox into thin strips and set aside.

2. Heat a large nonstick frying pan on medium-high heat. Add your butter and beaten eggs to the pan and stir continuously with a rubber spatula.

3. Once the eggs are about halfway cooked, about 1 minute, add the caramelized onions, crème fraîche, and salt and pepper to taste.

4. Once the eggs are softly scrambled, divide them among four plates.

5. Garnish the eggs with the julienned lox.

6. Serve with your choice of bagels or challah.

CREAM CHEESE TWO WAYS

I GREW UP EATING CREAM CHEESE at least twice a week. I gotta tell you, though, now that I'm in my mid-40s, my tastes have changed. On my bagel, I much prefer butter and lots of it. The perfect bagel for me is a double-toasted everything-spice bagel generously smeared with butter and topped with thinly sliced lemon, dill gravlax, and a bit of red onion. That's it. But for those of you who are still loyal to cream cheese, this recipe is for you.

2 cups	Elite cream cheese or another cream cheese if you prefer
4 to 5 OR	scallions, thinly sliced
3 Tbsp	prepared horseradish, well drained
1 Tbsp	fresh lemon juice

1. To a stand mixer with the paddle attachment, add your cream cheese and choice of scallions or horseradish and lemon juice.

2. Mix on medium-low speed for 1 to 2 minutes. Serve on whatever your heart desires!

[SCHMALTZ APPETIZING]

Bagels

Schmaltz Appetizing is an appetizing store. Schmaltz Appetizing is not a bagel store. We sell one type of bagel in a variety of flavors. If you would like to fight about this—my choice of bagel—please come down and take a number. By definition, appetizing stores sell things that go on and/or with bagels. Please come argue with me about Toronto bagels vs. Montreal bagels or New York bagels. I will win every time.

I absolutely love Montreal bagels. Ess-a-Bagel in New York is divine. I grew up on Gryfe's bagels and live and die for Kiva's bagels. But truth be told, I hardly ever eat bagels or bread or pasta or grains anymore. A few years ago I went strong paleo, so I eat a lot of meat, vegetables, nuts, and seeds. Once a week I go crazy and eat whatever I want. Mostly grease on grease or Five Guys, whichever is closer.

NOTE: Adding more Nutella to this recipe is not a bad idea. You can also pan-fry one of the loaf pieces on both sides, after it has been cooked, and top with more Nutella.

NUTELLA BABKA BREAD PUDDING

I STAND WITH ELAINE BENES (you know, Elaine from Seinfeld) on the great babka debate. Cinnamon babka is a lesser babka than chocolate babka. By a longshot. In this recipe, the sourness of the labneh and the sweetness of the maple syrup, combined with the crunch of the hazelnuts and the savoriness of the halvah, make for a mouth full of joy. It's also pretty cool to bring cuisines together like this. Maple syrup of Ontario, challah from my childhood, labneh and halvah from the Homeland. Yeah, pretty cool.

1/2 loaf	challah, homemade (page 65) or store-bought
	Unsalted butter, for greasing
1 cup	labneh or pressed plain Greek yogurt, for serving
1/4 cup	toasted, crushed hazelnuts, for serving
1	small piece halvah, grated, for serving
1/2 cup	maple syrup, for serving

CUSTARD:

2 cups	heavy cream (35%)
6	large eggs
1/2 Tbsp	vanilla paste or extract
1/2 tsp	kosher salt
2 1/2 Tbsp	brown sugar, well packed
5 Tbsp	white sugar
1/2 cup	Nutella or other chocolate-hazelnut spread

1. The night before you'd like to serve this, preheat the oven to 350°F and cut the challah into small cubes. Toast the challah on a baking sheet in the preheated oven until mostly dried throughout, about 20 minutes. If the bread is still quite soft, it won't absorb nearly as much of the custard.

2. For the custard, in a large bowl, combine the heavy cream, eggs, vanilla, salt, brown and white sugars, and Nutella. Using a hand mixer, blend the custard ingredients. Add the challah croutons to the bowl to soak in the custard overnight in the fridge.

3. The next day, preheat the oven to 350°F, grease a loaf pan with butter and line the bottom with parchment paper, and boil a kettle of water.

4. Transfer your bread pudding to the loaf pan, cover it with more parchment paper, and wrap with aluminum foil. Put the loaf pan in a larger casserole dish, then slowly pour the boiled water into the casserole dish until it comes about 1 inch up the sides of the loaf pan. Bake in the preheated oven for 1 to 1 1/2 hours, then remove to a wire rack to cool.

5. Once the loaf is just cool enough to handle, remove it from the pan and cut it into thick slices.

6. If you're serving this later, you can reheat it in the oven until it's just toasted and hot throughout. To serve, top with labneh, toasted hazelnuts, grated halvah, and maple syrup.

SWAN

A CROWD HAS GATHERED behind the steamy windows of Swan by Rose and Sons. The lights are dimmed, the music's cranked, and the place is already jammed by the time I walk into the busy, art-filled diner on this slushy winter night.

Anthony's invited some friends—an eclectic mix of food and fashion people, literary luminaries, artists, intellectuals, and stray weirdos—for the reveal of the restaurant's latest menu. This one is based on the concept of the meat and three, an obscure regional style of restaurant popular in the southern US. The meal features a choice of one meat: say, fried chicken, meatloaf, or ribs; and three sides: grits, collards, fried tomatoes, and such.

Swan's take on these southern classics means smoked pork rack with Chinatown fried rice, griddled mac and cheese, and Ezell's sweet slaw. It's not the first menu revamp for Swan, but it will prove to be the last.

The writing has been on the wall for Swan by Rose and Sons for a while, though on this night, it might be hard to see. Maybe it's covered by the Basquiat prints, or hidden behind the old Trans Am hood, or obscured by the swaths of commissioned graffiti. But in a career marked by a nearly unbroken string of success, Anthony will ultimately find Swan to be a painful, but educational failure.

"The original Swan diner was one of those classic Toronto places," he says. "It was never good, but it was always fantastic. It was a hangout for artists and musicians long before Queen Street was happening. Back in the 80s, before the Drake Hotel, before Trinity Bellwoods was a hipster paradise, and before the art galleries, Swan was there."

When word got out that the diner was for sale, it seemed like the kind of place tailor-made for Anthony.

"I was on a yoga retreat with my business partner, Rob, and his wife, Jackie, in Mexico when I heard about Swan," he says. "I wasn't supposed to be checking email, but somehow I got word that it was closing, so I got in touch with the owner right away. It seemed like the perfect fit. I mean, taking over classic old places and transforming them? That's what we do!"

He wasn't alone in feeling that Swan had something special. All of the city's top restaurateurs, and plenty of not-so-top ones, were looking at the space. With no time to spare, Anthony came back from Mexico and went directly to the restaurant to meet with the owner. "We had some friends in common," he says, "and one of his questions was 'What do you want to do with the space?' I said, 'I don't want to do anything, it's perfect,' and he said, 'Okay, it's yours.'"

Stoy.of SWan - old school restaurant

Unlike Fat Pasha, where the concept for the menu was agonized over, Anthony knew right away what he wanted the food to be at Swan. The restaurant would pay tribute to the formative years he spent learning to cook in California and the chefs out there who influenced him: Bradley Ogden, Jonathan Waxman, Mark Franz, and Jeremiah Tower.

"Swan was our fifth place, and I guess I was feeling nostalgic," he recalls. "California taught me to cook. Sure, I'd worked in places here in Toronto before that, but the kitchens I came up in were very old-school, lots of yelling, lots of screaming, lots of chefs throwing things. When I moved to California in 1993, I thought that's just how a kitchen had to be, but the thing is, it wasn't. It was very casual. Don't get me wrong, we worked really fucking hard, but there was respect."

The California Culinary Academy in San Francisco gave the 21-year-old cook his first serious academic exposure to cooking. Everything at school was based in traditional French standards—Escoffier, the classics. As part of his training, Anthony took an externship at the Mandarin Oriental Hotel, cooking the kind of California fusion food that was in fashion at the time, but it was his next two positions that really turned him on.

"I went to work with Bradley Ogden at the Lark Creek Inn," Anthony says, "which to me is still one of the most perfect restaurants in the world. You're sitting there in Marin County, eating your roast chicken with mashed potatoes and watching a family of deer roam through the creek. It's incredible." Following that, Anthony spent five years at San Francisco's influential Farallon restaurant under chef Mark Franz, who had previously been the chef at Stars with culinary legend, Jeremiah Tower. "I learned what California cuisine was at Farallon: simple food carefully prepared using mostly local ingredients in a modern way. That wasn't happening in Canada or the US at the time, and it was a really important change," Anthony says.

Fresh, local, and simple were the aesthetics Anthony brought to Swan, and for a while, it worked. "We started out strong," he says. "Breakfast and lunch were consistently busy, but dinner never seemed to happen. You can't pay the bills off $14-average checks. You're on Queen Street and it's expensive. We were drowning."

Then the review came out. A few months after Swan's opening, the Globe and Mail—Canada's leading national newspaper—published a punishing review of the restaurant, calling the place, among other things, "generally appalling." It was by far the worst review Anthony had ever received, and, he admits, "it kind of freaked me out."

"The worst thing I did at that point was change everything," he says. "We thought that we had to plug this hole or we'd drown. We made it more like Rose and Sons on Dupont, our original location, and that was a huge mistake. Instead of this idea of California cuisine, we went back to the same comfort food we were known for uptown. We should have kept on with what we were doing, just tweaking it and making it better. There was a lot of learning there. The most important thing I took away, regardless of all the bullshit, is that we just should have stayed the course."

It wasn't all bad, though, and for at least this one cold winter night, just a few months before Anthony will shut the place down for good, Swan by Rose and Sons achieves its full, glorious potential.

DJ Kaewonder is spinning classic New Orleans funk at a level louder than it should be. Identical-twin fashion journalists are schooling a wine importer on the finer points of asymmetric styling and the latest denim collabs. Art dealers Jason Halter and Carl Davis debate art authentication with a leading philosopher of social change. There's shaved meatloaf with mushroom gravy and hot chicken and bourbon.

It's everything Anthony wants in a restaurant: loud, fun, raucous, and delicious.

A few months later, shortly after he's sold the restaurant and moved on, I ask him about that night. "When Swan was on, it was the greatest restaurant in our group," he says. "The problem is it was hardly ever on. It was on maybe a dozen times in the months that we had it. Still, we learned a lot from Swan. We work our butts off at all the restaurants, but Swan just killed us. As soon as we sold it, we felt great. It was a huge relief. We lost money, but it taught us to stay true to our vision. It was the greatest lesson ever."

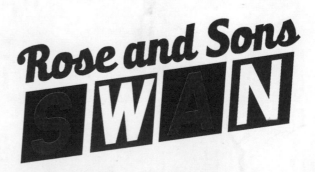

BUTTER LETTUCE SALAD

SERVES 2

THIS RECIPE, WITH ITS CALIFORNIA SENSIBILITIES, is from the menu from my first stab at Swan. I say "stab" here, as it's a good word to describe all the beautiful troubles we had at Swan. STAB STAB STAB STAB STAB. Ahhhhhhhh, better, thanks. Salad is good.

1 head	butter lettuce
1	red grapefruit
1	avocado
1/4 cup	ranch dressing (page 253)
1 Tbsp	poppy seeds

1. Carefully remove all the leaves of your butter lettuce individually. Wash them very gently in still water to avoid bruising, then dry them thoroughly on a paper towel.

2. You're going to build a butter lettuce mountain on a large serving plate. Start with the largest leaves on the bottom and gradually start piling up the smaller ones until you have a gorgeous butter lettuce mountain.

3. Slice the peel and pith off the top, bottom, and sides of the grapefruit so you can see the flesh. Run your knife between each wedge to separate the segment from the pith—now you have supremes. Place the grapefruit supremes evenly over the lettuce.

4. Peel, pit, and cut your avocado into 12 lengthwise slices and place them evenly on your salad.

5. Drizzle the ranch dressing overtop, then sprinkle with poppy seeds.

[SWAN]

131

COUNTRY GREEK

I MADE THE MISTAKE ONCE OF MAKING THIS SALAD, and now it's here in perpetuity.
I think I first made it at the Drake Hotel, but I showed it to my mother, Linda,
who can now make it in her sleep. It has always been and will remain a staple at
the cottage and at the restaurants. It's a perfect salad, and with the addition of
the chickpeas, it can be a meal on its own. Serve it with the JW Bird (page 18),
the Miami Ribs (page 241), or just by itself with a glass of rosé, and all the
Roses are happy.

1	English cucumber
1 pint	grape tomatoes, halved
1/2	red onion, diced small
1/2 cup	chopped kalamata olives
1 cup	cooked chickpeas, optional (see note)
1 tsp	kosher salt
1 tsp	dried Greek oregano
2 Tbsp	fresh lemon juice
1/4 cup	olive oil
1/2 cup	crumbled goat feta

1. Quarter the cucumbers lengthwise, then cut them into 3/4-inch pieces.

2. In a large bowl, mix the cucumbers with the tomatoes, onions, olives, and chickpeas (if using). Season with salt, oregano, and lemon juice. Let this marinate for about 10 minutes, mixing every couple of minutes.

3. Once the veg have marinated, add the olive oil and toss well to coat the salad.

4. Serve on a platter and cover with the crumbled feta.

NOTE: If you're using canned chickpeas, rinse them very well before adding to the salad. This salad is great with cold leftover grilled chicken or fish.

GUACAMOLE AND CHIPS

I HAVE THREE SIMPLE RULES to live by when making guacamole:

1. Do not use lime, baking soda, or citric acid or anything of the sort. The acid kills the guacamole and overshadows the creamy goodness of love in your mouth.
2. If someone is "allergic" to or hates cilantro, then they don't eat your guacamole. Hi Mom!!
3. Always ask for guacamole and chips as your last meal if you're on death row. Guacamole tacos with chicharróns is one of the best meals I have ever eaten. Thank you, Mexico City.

	Vegetable oil, for frying
12	large yellow corn tortillas
2 Tbsp	kosher salt, divided
4	ripe avocados
1/2 cup	small-diced red onions
1	jalapeño, finely diced and seeds removed
1/2 cup	chopped fresh cilantro

1. Prepare your deep fryer or a large pot and heat the oil to 365°F. A kitchen thermometer is useful here, and make sure to use enough oil so that the tortilla pieces can move around freely. Cut your tortillas into six equal pieces and fry in batches until golden and crispy, about 3 to 4 minutes. Don't overcrowd the fryer and make sure to let the oil come back up to temperature between batches. If you aren't going to fry your own tortillas, find a Latin American grocery store and buy their freshly made chips—if you're in Toronto, I recommend going to La Tortilleria.

2. Once the chips have cooked, remove them from the oil and place them on a plate lined with paper towel to drain any excess oil. Season with 1 Tbsp of salt.

3. For the guacamole, scoop out your avocados, place in a large bowl, and combine with the onions, jalapeños, cilantro, and the remaining kosher salt. Mash with a fork until it's as smooth or chunky as you like.

[SWAN]

WHOLE FISH SANDWICH

PURDY'S FISH MARKET IN SARNIA is wicked cool. We are so lucky to have so much
great freshwater fish in Ontario; however, most of the catch goes south of the
border to New York and beyond to make all that delicious gefilte fish (page 105).
If you can get your hands on some Ontario fish, try this recipe out. I'm a huge
supporter of nose-to-tail eating and cooking. Case in point: this sandwich. The
only things that go to waste are the pin bones. Plus, it looks just stunning.

	Vegetable oil, for frying
4	boneless perch or whitefish fillets
	Kosher salt and freshly ground black pepper
2 cups	buttermilk
4 cups	all-purpose flour
4 Tbsp	unsalted butter
4	hamburger buns
1/4 cup	tartar sauce (page 253)
2 cups	shredded iceberg or romaine lettuce
1	large tomato, sliced
1	lemon, quartered (optional)

1. Prepare your deep fryer or a large pot, and heat the oil to 365°F. A kitchen thermometer is useful here and make sure to use enough oil so that the fish has room to move around freely.

2. While the oil is heating, season your fish with salt and pepper and let sit for 10 minutes before breading. In the meantime, set up a dredging station. Place the buttermilk in a large shallow bowl, and place the flour in a separate shallow bowl.

3. Soak your fish in the buttermilk, one or two pieces at a time, for 1 minute each. Transfer the fish to the flour and coat it. If you're using the whole fish, make sure to bread it inside and out by opening up the body of the fish and getting the buttermilk and flour everywhere inside.

4. Drop your fish into the hot oil to fry for about 6 minutes. Remove the fish from the oil and place on a plate lined with paper towels to soak up the excess oil. Season lightly with salt.

5. Butter your hamburger buns and fry in a large pan over medium heat until golden, about 1 to 2 minutes.

6. To prepare the sandwiches, put tartar sauce on both the top and bottom buns. Put your fish on the bottom buns and top with shredded lettuce and a slice of tomato. This is also great with a squeeze of lemon. Close the sandwiches with the top buns and enjoy.

[SWAN]

Please, please, please brine this.

SMOKED PORK RACK WITH CHILIES

THE REASON WE SERVE a smoked pork chop as a side for breakfast is that on one of our many trips to Asheville to visit my ex-wife Kymberly's parents, we ate at the Moose Cafe. The waiter asked if I wanted bacon, sausage, a pork chop, country ham, or livermush as a side for my breakfast. I took it all. Please, please, please brine this. Whole big cuts like this one really need the tenderness that results from a bit of time in the brine.

BRINE:

6 Tbsp	kosher salt
6 Tbsp	brown sugar
10	juniper berries
10	bay leaves
1	pork rack (see note)
1 cup	pickled chilies (page 255)

1. For the brine, in a large pot, combine the salt, sugar, juniper berries, and bay leaves with 1 quart water. Bring it up to a boil, then as soon as it's boiling, pour it into a large container along with 3 quarts ice water to chill it immediately.

2. Submerge your pork rack into the brine and let it sit in the fridge for 2 to 3 days.

3. After a few days, remove your pork from the brine. If you have a smoker, prepare it according to the manufacturer's instructions and heat it to 225°F. Dry your pork rack well, and smoke it for 4 to 6 hours or until it has an internal temperature of 160°F. If you don't have a smoker, you can buy a presmoked pork rack at a butcher shop. Ask your butcher if you can pick it up fresh out of the smoker. If it's not freshly smoked, wrap it in aluminum foil and gently warm it in a 250°F oven for about 1 hour to get it hot inside.

4. Let your pork rest for 20 minutes after smoking. If you like, you can heat your barbecue on high, and char the pork for a few minutes after it has rested for some extra goodness. Cut it into chops and cover with pickled chilies. Serve immediately.

[SWAN]

Labatt 50

We sold very simple cocktails and good local craft beers at Swan, but beer was always king and my king of beers is Labatt 50. It is good beer, locally made but now not locally owned, and has the greatest, most legendary history. Serve this cold beer with a double shot of Canadian whisky to truly appreciate the pleasures of Canada.

NOTE: I don't like frenched chops/roasts because
it gets rid of so much juicy fat and goodness.
So don't buy them for this recipe.

NOTE: I say this serves four, but I can easily eat most of this myself, so I never have to worry about the double-dip etiquette.

FRIED CHICKEN AND SAUCES

ON ONE OF MY MANY ROAD TRIPS TO NORTH CAROLINA, we ate nothing but fried chicken the whole time. I think we had it a thousand times. Mrs. Rowe's Family Restaurant and Catering just off the interstate was a stupendous find for fried chicken. It took me a few tries to order right, though. The first try, I ordered what I thought was fried chicken, but what arrived was cold with gravy on it. "As it should be," according to the server at Mrs. Rowe's. Confused, I tried and tried again until we got it just right.

4	chicken drumsticks
4	whole chicken wings
4	chicken thighs
2 cups	brine from a jar of kosher pickles
2 cups	buttermilk
	Canola oil, for frying
	Kosher salt

CHICKEN DREDGE:

2 cups	all-purpose flour
1 1/2 cups	cornstarch
1 cup	rice flour
1/2 cup	cornmeal

SAGE PESTO:

3 bunches	fresh sage
1/2 bunch	fresh parsley
1 cup	olive oil
1 cup	small-cubed Parmigiano Reggiano (or Grana Padano or pecorino)
1 cup	whole walnuts
6 cloves	garlic, smashed
	Kosher salt

HONEY BUTTER HOT SAUCE (HBHS):

1 lb	unsalted butter
1 cup	honey
1 cup	Sriracha
1 Tbsp	kosher salt

1. Place your chicken in a large bowl, cover with the pickle brine, and soak in the fridge overnight. Drain and discard the brine, leaving the chicken in the bowl, and cover with the buttermilk to soak in the fridge for 1 hour before breading.

2. Prepare your deep fryer or a large pot and heat the oil to 365°F. A kitchen thermometer is useful here, and make sure to use enough oil so that the chicken can move around freely.

3. For the chicken dredge, in a large bowl, combine the flour, cornstarch, rice flour, and cornmeal. Transfer the chicken from the buttermilk to the dredge and coat well.

4. In batches if necessary, fry the chicken for 6 to 10 minutes. The chicken is cooked when it has reached an internal temperature of 165°F—make sure to check with a meat thermometer. Remove the chicken as it is ready: wings will be first and thighs will be last. Place the fried chicken on large plates lined with paper towel to soak up the excess oil, and sprinkle with salt to taste.

5. For the sage pesto, remove the stems from the sage and parsley and pulse in a food processor with the olive oil until it's roughly chopped. Add the Parmigiano Reggiano, walnuts, and garlic and pulse until chunky. Taste for seasoning and add salt to taste. Put in a jar and top with a bit of extra olive oil to avoid discoloration.

6. For the HBHS, melt the butter in a medium pan over medium heat, then whisk in the honey, Sriracha, and salt.

7. Serve the chicken with the dips on the side. Dip and double dip as you go.

[SWAN]

143

Pork Belly Fried Rice

PORK BELLY FRIED RICE

FARALLON IN SAN FRANCISCO was the first place I made this rice, though at first, I cooked it with Dungeness crab, fried shiitake mushrooms, and a sesame aioli instead of pork belly. The idea came from reading Eat Your Way across the U.S.A. by Jane and Michael Stern, an absolutely seminal text for anyone making a cross-country road trip.

1 Tbsp	kosher salt + extra for seasoning
3 cups	jasmine rice
2 lb	pork belly, boneless, skin on
2	large eggs
2 cups	broccoli florets
1/2 cup	canola oil
1/2 tsp	chili flakes
2 Tbsp	drained and julienned pickled ginger
	Freshly ground black pepper
1/4 cup	Ontario red-skinned peanuts
2	scallions, thinly sliced on a bias

CHINATOWN MARINADE:

2 cups	hoisin
1 cup	white sugar
1 Tbsp	Chinese five-spice powder
1 cup	low-sodium soy sauce
1 1/2 cups	rice wine vinegar
1/2 cup	sesame oil
10 cloves	garlic, smashed
1 bunch	scallions, roughly chopped

PICKLED SHIITAKE MUSHROOMS:

1 lb	shiitake mushroom caps, stems removed
1 cup	low-sodium soy sauce
1 cup	white sugar
1 cup	rice wine vinegar

1. Fried rice works best if you cook the rice a day ahead of when you want to eat it. Preheat the oven to 350°F. Bring 4 cups water and the salt to a boil in a large pot. As soon as the water has come to a boil, stir in the rice, cover with a lid, and put in the oven for 20 minutes. Once the rice is done, spread it out onto a baking sheet and transfer to the fridge to cool and dry out overnight.

2. You'll want to marinate your pork belly the day before as well. For the Chinatown marinade, in a container large enough to hold the belly, combine the hoisin, sugar, Chinese five-spice, soy sauce, rice wine vinegar, sesame oil, garlic, and scallions. Place the pork belly in the container and massage it with your hands to get it well coated with the marinade. Marinate in the fridge overnight.

3. The next day, remove the pork belly from the marinade and reserve the liquid. Preheat the oven to 350°F.

4. Dry off the pork belly, place in a roasting pan, and roast in the preheated oven for 1 to 1 1/2 hours until a knife slides in easily. Remove from the oven and allow the pork to cool in the pan until it has come to room temperature. If the skin is burnt, discard it, but otherwise keep it intact. Cut the cooked belly into 1-inch cubes and set aside for frying.

[SWAN]

5. Put the reserved marinade in a saucepot and gently reduce by half. Strain out all the bits of garlic and scallions and discard. This sauce can burn quickly, so make sure it doesn't reduce at a boil.

6. Next, prepare your shiitake mushrooms. In a large pot over medium heat, combine the mushrooms, soy sauce, sugar, and rice wine vinegar. Bring to a simmer and cook the mushrooms for 15 to 20 minutes. Remove the mushrooms and let cool. Once cool, slice and they're ready to use.

7. Beat your eggs in a small bowl, then cook them in a small nonstick pan over low heat. Spread the eggs out over the pan so they look like crepes. Cook for 1 minute per side, then remove from the pan, slice into long strips, and set aside.

8. Blanch or steam your broccoli florets for about 1 minute, then cool in an ice-water bath for at least 2 minutes. Remove from the water and dry thoroughly on a towel. Set aside.

9. Get two large frying pans (nonstick if you'd like) smoking hot. Divide your canola oil and pork belly between the two pans and fry until crispy on all sides. I like to use two pans for this because you can't crowd the belly or the rice; they won't fry up properly if crowded.

10. Once the belly is crispy, divide the cooked rice and add it to the pans. Spread the rice into a thin layer and fry for 2 minutes without moving the rice too much.

11. When you're ready to start tossing the rice, add the chili flakes, pickled ginger, and broccoli to the pans. Check the seasoning and add salt and pepper to taste. Let cook for another 5 minutes or so until the rice is really crispy and delicious.

12. To serve, divide the rice evenly into bowls and garnish with peanuts, egg strips, pickled shiitakes, and scallions. Drizzle the reduced marinade liberally overtop.

[SWAN]

NOTE: You can do this with shrimp instead of pork, or with shrimp and pork for more of a good thing.

RED VELVET CAKE

THIS RECIPE COMES FROM CAKE MAN RAVEN, and I've been using it for years—I think it's one of the most perfect recipes in the world. I've used it as standard red velvet cake, and used it as the base for whoopie pies and pancakes as well. According to Saveur, "Red velvet cake was invented in the 1950s at Oscar's in New York's Waldorf-Astoria. However, Raven Dennis of Cake Man Raven Confectionery . . . claims red velvet cake originated during the Civil War, and that Southern ladies made it 'to keep their husbands home.'" I'm not sure where red velvet cake originated, but Cake Man Raven's is the best there is.

2 1/2 cups	all-purpose flour
1 1/2 cups	white sugar
1 tsp	baking soda
1 tsp	fine salt
1 tsp	cocoa powder
1 1/2 cups	vegetable oil
1 cup	buttermilk, room temperature
2	large eggs, room temperature
2 Tbsp	red food coloring
1 tsp	white vinegar
1 tsp	vanilla extract

CREAM CHEESE FROSTING:

16 oz	cream cheese, room temperature
1/2 cup	unsalted butter, room temperature
4 cups	icing sugar
2 tsp	vanilla extract
2 cups	crushed pecans, for garnish

1. Preheat the oven to 350°F.

2. In a large bowl, sift together the flour, sugar, baking soda, salt, and cocoa powder.

3. In a separate bowl, using a hand mixer, whisk together the oil and buttermilk. Mix in the eggs one at a time, then mix in the food coloring, vinegar, and vanilla.

4. Mix the dry ingredients into the wet by hand with a wooden spoon, just until a batter forms. Be careful not to overmix.

5. Lightly grease two 8-inch round baking pans. Lay a strip of parchment paper down in each pan to help remove the baked cakes more easily.

6. Divide the batter evenly between the two pans. Bake for 35 to 40 minutes or until a toothpick inserted into the center comes out clean. Cool the cakes on a rack until they come to room temperature, then remove the cakes from the pans.

7. For the frosting, in a large bowl, mix the cream cheese and butter together with a hand mixer until smooth. Mix in the icing sugar 1 cup at a time, mixing well between each addition. Mix in the vanilla.

8. Spread one-quarter of the frosting on one of the cooled cakes, then top with the second cake. Spread another quarter of the frosting on top, and spread the remaining frosting on the sides of the cakes. Garnish with pecans.

[SWAN]

BAR BEGONIA

FOR SUCH A DISTINGUISHED and venerable viticultural organization, the Confrérie des Chevaliers du Tastevin sure does have a silly dance. "La la la la," sing the men, waving their hands around and clapping to a simple rhythm. "La la la la."

The Confrérie (Fraternity of Knights of the Wine-Tasting Cup) is an exclusive international group of men and women, but mostly men, who have a near-obsessive passion for the wines of Burgundy. They're kind of like the Cub Scouts, except instead of activity badges, they live for some of the most expensive and sought-after wines in the world.

I'm not a Chevalier, but I'm crashing one of their parties tonight. Anthony invited me to join a dinner he's hosting for a local group of Chevaliers, including his father, Joel, who meet up like this every so often to uncork a few phenomenal wines, eat some delicious food, and sing a little song. We've all gathered, along with some of our best bottles, at Bar Begonia, Anthony's sexy little spaceship of a Parisian cocktail bar.

Sitting here at this marble table, eating warm oysters in a pool of smoked cream, and drinking Laurent-Perrier Grand Siècle Champagne out of handblown crystal, it's hard to believe that just a few short years ago, this same elegant space was an abandoned wreck.

"Bar Begonia was a broke-down palace when we first came across it," Anthony recalls. "It was musty. It was old. It was filthy. It was disgusting.

"The landlord said, 'We're looking for an injection of money and we'll build to suit, so just give us a million dollars and we'll take care of the rest.' Every restaurateur in the city must have looked at that space, but given the offer, everyone just walked away."

The idiosyncratic, staggered triplex of a building remained empty for years, earning a reputation as one of the neighborhood's biggest eyesores. Finally, a new lease sign came back up a few years later and Anthony and Rob decided to put their names in the running again. This time, the building's owners came back to them right away. The owners had done a lot of work cleaning the place up, putting in new drywall and new floors, and generally making it an inhabitable structure.

"The space finally worked, so we agreed to take it," Anthony says. "At first, we wanted to make it more of a Parisian cocktail bar, specifically because we don't have a huge cocktail program. The only problem was, we don't do bars. We do restaurants, we do food. The menu grew out of our take on classic French cooking in support of the cocktails."

The shelves behind the giant curved bar are filled with colorful bottles, the lighting is tuned to a flattering glow, and the walls are adorned with larger-than-life contour drawings of frolicking women.

There's an obvious erotic vibe to the place, but even more so in the name. Begonia, in addition to being a lovely and feminine word, has another, more specific meaning to the Rose family. "Begonia was always the nickname for a certain special female body part in my family growing up," Anthony says. "My nieces still crack up every time it's mentioned."

If Anthony's father is aware of this alternative definition for the restaurant, he doesn't let on over the course of our Chevaliers dinner. The meal follows a specific and time-honored set of rules. Bottles are carefully wrapped so no labels show. Glasses are poured just prior to the arrival of each course, and guests weigh in with their guesses on region, producer, vintage, and quality before pairing the wine with the food.

"We've been doing these dinners for years," Anthony's father, Joel, tells me. "The organizer sets up the dinner, tells us to bring a bottle, and nobody has a clue. He might say to bring a white burgundy or an Austrian grüner, but the best ones are when there's no theme. You just bring a bottle that you like, as long as it's interesting."

"Nobody would dare bring anything that was less than exceptional," one of the other Chevaliers explains.

My career has taken me to many of the world's great wine regions and I've had the opportunity to taste some pretty special wines, but not many meals in my experience have contained this many incredible wines in one sitting.

There's the Domaine Latour-Giraud Champ Canet, Puligny-Montrachet (one taster calls it "explosive"), and poached halibut in a light broth with fava beans, peas, and white asparagus with Parisian gnocchi. A rare 1966 Pierre Ponnelle Vosne Romanée premier cru ("still kicking") is paired with the duck ballotine stuffed with morels in foie gras sauce.

My selection, a 10-year-old Napa cabernet sauvignon from Dunn Vineyards, would be a meal's highlight on any other night. But tonight, it seems like a mere baby in this company, though it manages to hold its own against the epic côte de boeuf with summer truffle jus and poached leeks.

Although these Chevaliers are among the city's leading experts on the subject of wine, there's a candid honesty about the limits of high-end tasting. Still, it's something of a surprise when one of them turns to me and says, "It's all a scam."

"What is?" I ask.

"These tastings where you have these masters of wine sit down and proceed to identify exactly what wine it is. It's all a scam," he says. "There's a game going on here. As soon as you draw a circle around these wines, say you're doing Left Bank bordeaux, and you taste one, it doesn't take much experience to be able to say, this is quite old. This is older than 30, maybe pushing 40 or 50 years. All of a sudden, you've narrowed things down dramatically. If you know it's more than 30 years old, there's only three vintages in Left Bank bordeaux that could possibly, at this point in time, taste really delicious."

"So it takes only 20 years of experience drinking the best vintages of the best wine from around the world, and suddenly it all makes sense," I say. "Exactly," he replies.

"The funny thing about these dinners," says Joel, "is the feeling of absolute and complete idiocy you have at the end of the evening when you leave, as not only did you not pick out what anybody else's wine is, you didn't even spot your own."

As the meal winds down, a tarte au chocolat is presented along with glasses of 40-year-old port. I tell Anthony I always knew he was into wine, but didn't know he was Montrachet Grand Cru into wine.

"Wine was a big part of growing up for me," he says. "Our family trips were always built around traveling and eating. My parents would bring us everywhere: Michelin-starred restaurants in Europe where they'd serve jelly aspics at lunch. No North American kid was meant to be there. I feel privileged to have had those experiences, but it's not at all the kind of thing I aspire to. Begonia might be the most formal and classic of my restaurants, but it's still relaxed and, hopefully, fun."

I tell Anthony I always knew he was into wine

PIERRE PONNELLE
1966

2013

but didn't know he was Montrachet Grand Cru into wine.

GOUGÈRES

THIS RECIPE WAS INFLUENCED BY JUDY RODGERS at Zuni Café. While I lived in San Francisco, Zuni was my go-to with my wife at the time, by myself, and especially when my parents came to visit. I actually had the opportunity to work there a couple of times, but always preferred eating there to working there and wanted to keep that magic to myself. Zuni is one of my all-time perfect restaurants and one that I continue to get so much influence from every day.

8	large eggs
1/2 lb	unsalted butter
1/2 tsp	kosher salt
1 tsp	white sugar
1 3/4 cups	all-purpose flour
1 cup	grated gruyère
1/2 bunch	fresh chives, finely chopped

1. Preheat the oven to 400°F and bring your eggs out of the fridge to come to room temperature.

2. Put the butter, 2 cups water, and the salt and sugar in a medium pot and bring up to a boil, then turn down to a simmer.

3. Add the flour and stir constantly with a wooden spoon. This will need to be stirred vigorously for at least 5 minutes to make sure that the choux is cooked. There will be some flour stuck to the pot once it's done.

4. Add the hot choux and cheese to a stand mixer with the paddle attachment and mix on medium-low speed. Add the eggs one at a time, mixing until they're fully incorporated before adding the next egg. Finally, add your chives and mix for 10 more seconds.

5. Once the dough has come together, transfer it to a piping bag fitted with a medium round tip. Line a baking sheet with parchment paper and pipe out 1-inch balls onto the prepared sheet, about 2 inches apart. You may have to do this in batches on multiple baking sheets. If you don't have a piping bag, you can just dollop the batter with a tablespoon, which will give the final product a rustic look.

6. Bake in the preheated oven for 15 minutes, rotate the baking sheet, and bake for 10 more minutes.

7. When the gougères are done, they will have doubled in size and feel hollow and light. Serve warm.

ENDIVE SALAD

THIS IS PROBABLY ONE OF THE LIGHTER, more refreshing dishes I have ever made in my life. This dressing could have a few pink and/or green peppercorns in it to put it over the top. I like a ton of slivered almonds, well toasted, and a huge showering of tarragon as well. The inner part of the endive heart, closest to the base and so very bitter, is like magic to me.

4	large Belgian endives
2	red grapefruits, segmented and supremed (page 131)
1/2 bunch	fresh tarragon, leaves only
1/4 cup	slivered almonds, toasted

LEMON VINAIGRETTE:

2 Tbsp	fresh lemon juice
1 Tbsp	dijon mustard
6 Tbsp	olive oil
	Pinch of kosher salt

1. Cut the bottoms off of the endives and separate the leaves. Pile the leaves in an endive mountain, with the largest leaves at the bottom and the smallest at the top.

2. Scatter your grapefruit segments over the salad, followed by the tarragon and slivered almonds.

3. For the vinaigrette, in a small bowl, combine the lemon juice, mustard, olive oil, and salt. Blend well with a whisk or an immersion blender.

4. Lightly dress the salad with the lemon vinaigrette and drizzle any excess grapefruit juice overtop as well.

The Birth of Begonia

It's funny that all of my restaurants have a personal origin story of deep meaning to my life and eating habits. All except Bar Begonia. I could say that my time at either Farallon with Mark Franz or Mercer Kitchen with Jean-Georges Vongerichten influenced me with French flavors or ideas. Or that going to the California Culinary Academy in San Francisco, which was so old-school and steeped in French education, was on my mind. But no, none of those were the reason I wanted to create Begonia. I think I just loved the idea of doing something so old-school and classic. French bistro, based on the classics of butter and ham with hints of madeira and rosé, was all I wanted. However, if anyone asks, I always tell them that I lived in Paris and wanted to recreate all my memories of my favorite haunts. Not completely untrue; I did live in Paris on three separate occasions for a week at a time. On vacation.

THIS RECIPE ALWAYS BRINGS
ME BACK TO WHEN I WAS A

Cowboy.

STEAK TARTARE

THIS RECIPE ALWAYS BRINGS ME BACK to when I was a cowboy for a day at the ranch of Chef Emily Luchetti's family, north of Napa Valley. I lassoed, dehorned, castrated, branded, and injected the cows with antibiotics. I wore jeans, cowboy boots, a cowboy hat, and a green bandana. At the end of the day, we cooked for the (real) cowboys a feast that included all the castrated balls soaked in buttermilk, dredged in cornmeal, and panfried over an open fire. This recipe isn't quite as rugged as what we made that day, but you'll feel like a rugged cowboy or cowgirl nonetheless.

1 lb	beef tenderloin, or another good-quality piece of beef from your butcher
4 tsp	dijon mustard
10 dashes	Worcestershire
10 dashes	Tabasco
2 Tbsp	finely chopped capers
2 Tbsp	finely chopped cornichons or dill pickles
5 tsp	finely minced shallots
1/2 bunch	fresh parsley, finely chopped
	Kosher salt and freshly ground black pepper
4	very fresh large egg yolks
	Potato chips, for garnish

1. Remove any excess fat or sinew from your tenderloin. With a very sharp knife, thinly slice the beef, cut the slices into thin strips, and finally chop the strips into very small cubes. You want all the pieces to be the same size and cut cleanly, without any ragged edges.

2. In a large bowl, mix the beef with the mustard, Worcestershire, Tabasco, capers, cornichons, shallots, and parsley. Taste for seasoning and adjust with salt and pepper.

3. Divide the tartare among four bowls and make a well in the middle of the meat with the back of a spoon. Carefully place an egg yolk in each well.

4. Garnish each bowl with a good helping of potato chips. Let guests break up the egg yolk and mix it in just before eating.

[BAR BEGONIA]

OMELETTE À LA PÉPIN

THE FIRST TIME I MET JACQUES PÉPIN, he was with Julia Child at Farallon in
San Francisco. They came into the kitchen to say thanks for a special dinner we had
made for them. I remember Julia saying something to me that, for the life of me,
I just couldn't understand. Maybe it was her accent, but I just couldn't get it.
After the third time of me nodding and smiling in answer to the same question,
Jacques finally piped in and said, "She wants to know where you're from." Anyway,
I got that going for me.

3	oeufs
1/2 tsp	kosher salt
2 tsp	herbes fines (a combo of finely chopped fresh parsley, chives, and tarragon)
1 Tbsp	unsalted butter

1. In a bowl and using a fork, beat your oeufs, salt, and herbes fines. Work in a small, swirly, scrambling motion.

2. Heat an 8-inch nonstick pan over medium heat. Once the pan is warm, add your butter.

3. When the butter has just melted, pour your eggs into the pan.

4. Allow the eggs to set and curl at the edges.

5. Using the tines of your fork, stir the runny parts of the omelet, allowing the uncooked egg to fall into the exposed parts of the pan. Continue this until the eggs are mostly set but still creamy and liquid inside.

6. Fold a third of the omelet in toward the middle, then fold it again and turn it out onto a plate with the folded seam down.

[BAR BEGONIA]

NOTE: My classic omelet should not be stuffed with anything. Wild mushrooms sautéed in butter or truffles on top of the omelet would be fine, though.

LE GRAND AIOLI

WHEN I LIVED IN PARIS (see page 162), this was one of my favorite dishes to eat. I love the simple preparation, the abundance and variety, and the final elegant presentation of deliciousness. Also, it's paleo, so I eat it all the time. Keep in mind that this trout needs 12 hours to cure, so it's best to start this recipe ahead of time.

MI-CUIT TROUT:

8 oz	steelhead trout, filleted, skin removed
1 tsp	kosher salt
1/2 tsp	white sugar
2 Tbsp	olive oil

COURT BOUILLON:

1/2 head	fennel, roughly chopped
1/2 head	celery, roughly chopped
1	white onion, roughly chopped
4	bay leaves
1	lemon, halved
1 cup	white wine
2 Tbsp	kosher salt
1 Tbsp	black peppercorns

PICKLED BEETS:

2 lb	golden beets
1 cup	cider vinegar
1/2 cup	white sugar
1 Tbsp	kosher salt
2	bay leaves

AIOLI:

2	large egg yolks
1	large clove garlic, minced
2 tsp	dijon mustard
4 tsp	fresh lemon juice
	Pinch of kosher salt
1/4 cup	olive oil
1/4 cup	canola oil

FOR SERVING:

4	raw radishes, quartered
3	large hard-boiled eggs, quartered
	Raw hen-of-the-woods mushrooms
	An assortment of green beans, broccoli, and baby carrots, blanched and cooled
	Crusty bread

1. To make the mi-cuit trout, portion your trout into four equal 2 oz chunks. Season with the salt and sugar and place in a resealable container. Cure covered in the fridge for at least 8 hours.

2. The next day, prepare your court bouillon. In a large pot, combine the fennel, celery, onions, bay leaves, lemon halves, wine, salt, and peppercorns. Add 6 quarts water and bring up to a simmer over medium-high heat for at least 30 minutes. After 30 minutes, strain the bouillon, return it to the pot, and heat it to 45°F. A kitchen thermometer is essential here. Gently lay your trout portions into the poaching liquid and poach for 45 minutes. Make sure your liquid stays at a consistent temperature or you may overcook your fish. If you have a sous-vide cooker, you can skip making the court bouillon and simply place your trout portions in a vacuum bag with the olive oil, seal, and sous vide for 45 minutes.

3. To make the pickled beets, in a small pot, combine the beets, cider vinegar, sugar, salt, and bay leaves with 1 cup water. Use as small a pot as possible to make sure that the beets are covered in the liquid.

4. Simmer the beets over medium heat until a knife goes in with little resistance. This could take 40 to 60 minutes depending on the size of your beets. Allow the beets to cool, then peel and cut them into 1-inch chunks.

5. To make the aioli, combine the egg yolks, garlic, mustard, lemon juice, and salt in a food processor. Turn the processor on and mix for a few seconds to aerate the ingredients. Then, with the processor still running, slowly drizzle in the oils to emulsify your aioli. Taste and add seasoning if needed.

6. To serve, make small piles of the trout, pickled beets, radishes, eggs, mushrooms, green beans, broccoli, and carrots around the plate. Use a little bit of this, and a little bit of that. I like a smaller plate, so it looks full with goodness. Put the aioli in a deep ramekin on top of the whole mountain of glory. Serve with crusty bread, if desired.

MUSHROOMS ON TOAST WITH BRANDY CREAM

AT WASHINGTON PARK IN NEW YORK, Jonathan Waxman served sweetbreads with mushrooms in a buttery, buttery madeira sauce. We panfried the breaded sweetbreads in butter first, followed by a good glug of liquor and then loads more butter. This is that, but with eggs. And on toast. I love Jonathan Waxman so much.

2 Tbsp	canola oil
1 cup	cremini mushrooms, halved
1 cup	hen-of-the-woods mushrooms
1 tsp	chopped fresh thyme
2 Tbsp	brandy
1/2 cup	heavy cream (35%)
	Kosher salt and freshly ground black pepper
1 Tbsp	unsalted butter
1 Tbsp	finely chopped fresh chives
	Your favorite sourdough
1	large egg

1. Heat a large pan on high until it's very hot. Don't use cast iron for this. When you start to see a bit of smoke coming from your pan, you know it's ready.

2. Add the canola oil, then add your mushrooms right away and quickly move them around to absorb the oil. Keep moving and frying your mushrooms on high heat until you have good caramelization everywhere, about 1 to 2 minutes. Then add your chopped thyme.

3. When the shrooms are ready, add the brandy and stand back for a second in case it flames up.

4. Once any flames have subsided, add your cream, mix to combine, and let it come up to a bubble for 1 minute. Make sure the mixture is consistent.

5. Add salt and pepper to taste, then finish with butter and chives.

6. Toast your sourdough. While it toasts, fry an egg sunny-side up in a small nonstick pan.

7. Spoon the mushrooms and the creamy goodness over the toast, and top with the fried egg.

NOTE: Leftover duck confit can be picked away from the bone and heated up in its own fatty skin. Eat it with scrambled eggs or in a sandwich from Jesus.

DUCK CONFIT WITH SWEET POTATO GRATIN

SERVES 4

AS FAR AS I CAN REMEMBER, the first time I saw duck salt was at the Lark Creek Inn in Larkspur, California. I was a recent cooking-school grad and the French Laundry didn't want me. That was fine; my second choice turned out to be the best choice, because I met Mark Franz, who was just coming to Lark Creek after running Stars with Jeremiah Tower forever. I use duck salt on almost anything as a seasoning, but for curing duck legs, it's the fucking game winner. Start this recipe the night before you'd like to eat it so the duck has time to cure.

4	fatty duck legs
4	tsp duck salt (page 250)
4 to 8 cups	duck fat, depending on the size of your pot

SWEET POTATO GRATIN:

5 Tbsp	unsalted butter, divided
1 lb	russet potatoes
1 lb	sweet potatoes
2 cloves	garlic, finely minced
2 cups	heavy cream (35%)
3 Tbsp	white wine
2 dashes	Tabasco
1/4 bunch	fresh thyme
1 Tbsp	kosher salt
1 tsp	freshly ground black pepper
1/8 tsp	grated fresh nutmeg
1 cup	grated gruyère

1. Season your duck legs with the duck salt. Place them in a resealable container, cover, and let them sit in the fridge overnight to cure a bit.

2. The next day, preheat your oven to 300°F.

3. In a large straight-sided pot or Dutch oven, melt your duck fat over low heat until fully melted.

4. Add your duck legs to the fat and make sure that as much of the duck legs are covered as possible.

5. Put a lid on top of your pot or wrap it in aluminum foil. Put in the oven to confit for about 1 1/2 hours.

6. When your duck legs are done, most of the skin and meat should have receded up the shin toward the thigh and the meat should be tender throughout.

7. For the sweet potato gratin, preheat your oven to 400°F and grease an 8- x 8-inch baking pan with 1 Tbsp butter.

8. Peel both the russet and sweet potatoes, then slice them widthwise about 1/8 inch thick.

9. In a large pot over medium heat, place the potato slices, garlic, cream, wine, Tabasco, thyme, salt, pepper, and nutmeg and stir to combine. Keep stirring often with a wooden spoon for about 8 minutes. Once the potatoes have started to soften, stir in the remaining 4 Tbsp butter.

10. Transfer the potato mixture to the prepared baking pan and remove the thyme stems. Taste for seasoning and adjust as needed.

11. Press the potatoes into the pan as flat as possible, then cover with the grated gruyère and bake, uncovered, for 20 to 30 minutes until golden brown. Serve hot with the duck legs.

[BAR BEGONIA]

It's the fucking game winner.

DAVID CHOW'S STICKY TOFFEE PUDDING

DAVID CHOW IS ONE OF THE MOST gifted pastry chefs I have ever worked with. We first cooked together at the Drake Hotel in Toronto. This is his recipe, and it's perfect and delicious, just like him. At Bar Begonia, we add some yellow chartreuse to the brown-butter sauce to make a French version of his classic recipe.

1/2 lb	dried pitted dates, chopped
1 1/2 cups	coffee
1 tsp	baking soda
1/2 cup	unsalted butter
2 cups	icing sugar
2	large eggs
3 cups	all-purpose flour
1/2 tsp	grated fresh ginger
1/2 tsp	fine kosher salt
1 tsp	baking powder

CANDIED PECANS:

2 cups	pecans, untoasted
1/4 cup	maple syrup
2 tsp	honey
	Ground cinnamon, to taste
	Cayenne pepper, to taste
	Ground ginger, to taste
	Pinch of kosher salt and freshly ground black pepper

TOFFEE SAUCE:

1/2 lb	unsalted butter
2 cups	heavy cream (35%)
3 cups	brown sugar
1 tsp	kosher salt
	Splash of vanilla extract
2 Tbsp	yellow chartreuse
	Crème fraîche (recipe below or store-bought), for serving

1. To make the cake, preheat the oven to 350°F and line a 9- x 13-inch baking pan with parchment paper. Set out a larger roasting pan that can hold the baking pan with room around it for a water bath.

2. In a medium pot, combine the dates with the coffee and 1/2 cup water, and boil until the dates are somewhat softened, about 10 minutes.

3. Add the baking soda to the date mixture and let it sit until fully cooled. Puree the mixture with a hand mixer and set aside.

4. In a stand mixer, cream the butter and icing sugar together. Then, with the mixer running on low speed, add the eggs to the mixer one at a time. Add the dates to the butter-sugar mixture and mix to combine.

5. Slowly add the flour, ginger, salt, and baking powder to the wet ingredients and mix until just combined.

6. Pour the batter into the prepared baking pan, cover tightly with aluminum foil, and place the pan inside the larger roasting pan. Very carefully pour water into the roasting pan until it reaches halfway up the sides of the baking pan. Make sure that it doesn't splash into the cake.

7. Bake in the preheated oven for 1 hour or until the cake is firm to the touch. When the cake is done, remove from the oven but leave the oven on.

[BAR BEGONIA]

8. While the cake bakes, prepare your candied pecans. Line a baking sheet with parchment paper. In a large bowl, toss the pecans with the maple syrup and honey, just enough so that they're coated. Add the cinnamon, cayenne pepper, ginger, salt, and pepper to taste. Transfer the pecans to the prepared baking sheet. Once the cake is out of the oven, roast the pecans for 6 minutes, stirring every minute or so, until toasted. Let them cool, then coarsely chop and set aside.

9. Next, prepare the toffee sauce. In a large pot over low heat, brown the butter, watching carefully so it doesn't burn. Once the butter has browned, add the cream in a slow and steady stream—watch out for splatter.

10. Add the brown sugar to the butter and bring the mixture to a boil. Finally, add the salt, vanilla, and chartreuse, and stir to combine. Keep in mind that if the mixture boils for too long, it will separate. If that happens, simply re-emulsify it with an immersion blender.

11. While the cake is still warm, use a wooden skewer to poke holes in the top, then carefully pour the toffee sauce over the cake, allowing it to soak in. Serve each slice of cake with a dollop of crème fraîche and a scattering of candied pecans.

CRÈME FRAÎCHE

MAKES ABOUT 4 QUARTS

1 1/2 quarts	heavy cream (35%)
2 cups	buttermilk
	Splash of fresh lemon juice

1. Combine all the ingredients in a container and leave covered at room temperature for 2 days until thickened.

2. Strain through cheesecloth for a few hours until the desired consistency is reached.

NOTE: All components of this cake can be made ahead of time, and the cake/toffee can be reheated in the microwave or the oven in a covered pan. At the Drake, we combined the cake and toffee ahead of time into single-serving "packages," allowing the sauce to soak even more into the cakes.

Hemingway
AND I ARE VERY SIMILAR.

THE SUN ALSO RISES

HEMINGWAY AND I ARE VERY SIMILAR, or so I've been told. This novel, like my restaurants, is a roman à clef. My restaurants are based on real people, and the food and atmosphere are based on real events, but you might find some fictionalized aspects if you look closely. Just like Ernest.

1 oz	gin
1 oz	tangerine or mandarin orange juice
1/2 oz	grenadine
1 Tbsp	Pernod pastis
3 oz	sparkling wine

1. Combine the gin, tangerine juice, grenadine, and pastis in a cocktail shaker. Shake, then pour into a coupe glass and top with sparkling wine.

MADAME BOEUF

THE SCENE AT MADAME BOEUF this afternoon looks a bit like a dress rehearsal for a touring company production of Hair. Anthony is sporting a full-length fur coat—coyote, by the looks of it—and a cowboy hat. A pair of half-drunk lovers are playing a cutthroat game of corn hole without ever putting down their drinks. A gang of semi-feral children are running around shooting each other with an old pop gun. The Bee Gees are playing on the stereo.

Today, the first warm day of spring, is the inauguration of the flea market, an occasional bonus component of the whole Madame Boeuf backyard-burger-joint-and-ice-cream-dispensary experience. Half the picnic tables are covered in baskets of cheese fries, banquet burgers, and glasses of frozé (rosé wine that's been put through the slushie machine, natch). The other half are pressed into service as display tables for a seriously eclectic bunch of old junk: a rack of antlers, a suitcase full of kitsch paintings (cats in space sort of stuff), whisks and strainers galore, a stack of zines. Are there vintage Dr. Hook, Fleetwood Mac, and Michael McDonald records? Oh, yes. Plenty.

There's also a small bake sale that's generating a lot of excitement: delicious sourdough from Badass Breads, bakerman bars from Big Crow, cinnamon buns from Fat Pasha, peanut butter chocolate bars from Schmaltz.

At one point, Anthony's business partner, Rob, gets up on a picnic table and starts auctioning off a butter-tart pie his sister-in-law made that had been sitting around for a while and was in danger of melting in the sun. He actually manages a respectable $25 on the pie, but when I ask him about it after, he tells me, "I'm pretty sure she spent more than that making it. Our costs were really high on that pie."

For all of the entertaining distractions, though, Madame Boeuf is all about the burger, and no burger is more important to the Boeuf than the banquet burger. Ask anyone who grew up in Toronto what a banquet burger is, and they'll tell you it's a Toronto invention. They'll dispute who invented it, but all will insist it's a Toronto invention.

Ask someone who didn't grow up in Toronto, like me, what a banquet burger is, and they'll say, "What's that?"

The Toronto person will respond: "It's a burger with bacon and cheese. It was invented in Toronto."

"That's a bacon cheeseburger," the right-thinking, nonnative Torontonian will say. "That's a common thing."

"Nope," the Torontonian will reply. "It was invented at . . ." and then they will say some local burger joint: Fran's, Burger Shack, some long-forgotten greasy spoon.

There's no point arguing with them. As far as Torontonians are concerned, the idea of putting bacon on a cheeseburger originated right here in the city and is called a banquet burger.

As a Torontonian through and through, Anthony also totally believes this. "The banquet burger is a southern Ontario thing," he says. "Only people in Toronto can understand a banquet burger."

I'm not making this up.

"Growing up eating in shitty restaurants, the only thing I wanted was a burger with cheese and bacon," says Anthony. "Cheese and bacon. I don't know where it comes from. I've done some research, but the information is just not there. There's not really an origin story to the banquet. Fran's might be the originator. I'd go to Fran's as a kid; it would sometimes be the first and last stop of our night. This woman who had been working there for 30 years saw us coming and knew right away what we wanted, a banquet burger platter—the platter came with fries—and a side of onion rings. It was amazing."

"This is turning out just how I'd hoped," Anthony tells me as I'm in the middle of stuffing an onion ring into my mouth. "I really wanted this place to be something very accessible not only for adults, but for families and kids. If you're here early on some nights, it's like a family back here, the kids are throwing bocce and running around. The simplicity back here is beautiful."

Simple and beautiful it may be, but the origin of the banquet burger is not the only controversy surrounding Madame Boeuf.

Of all things, it is the restaurant's mascot, an illustrated lady of ample proportions engaged in a kind of semi-pinup pose grasping a massive burger, that has caused the most consternation. "I got a lot of flack for the image of Madame Boeuf that looks over the restaurant," Anthony says. "The overall management team was against it. I was dumbfounded. The piece was painted by Marta McKenzie, an artist I've wanted to work with for ages. She's classically trained and I consider her up there with Spiegelman and Crumb. Anyway, I look at it as a piece of art and I think she's beautiful. Sometimes when you have an idea that you like but everyone else hates, you just have to follow your heart."

The Hamburger:
ONE OF THE MOST
IMPORTANT FOOD GROUPS.

LE HAMBURGER

WE ALWAYS HAD MULTIPLE GRILLS in our house growing up. The one inside was gas and the one outside was charcoal. Even at the cottage, we had both gas and charcoal grills. Hardcore Canadians grill year-round, and we were no exception. It takes much longer at -30°C, but whisky makes everything easier. Even at Big Crow, which essentially is a year-round outdoor grill house, it gets pretty cold, but we prevail. Of course, the hamburger—one of the most important food groups—is a grill staple. I used to pile my burgers high with all the goods. At this point in my life, I'm pretty much a mustard and onion guy. Simple pleasures.

ROSEMARY HONEY BUTTER MAYO:

1/2 lb	unsalted butter
1/8 cup	honey
1/2 bunch	fresh rosemary, finely chopped
1 1/2 cups	mayo
1 dash	Tabasco
2 tsp	kosher salt
10 oz	good-quality ground beef chuck, made into two equal patties (see note)
	Kosher salt and freshly ground black pepper
2 (3-inch)	classic hamburger buns, sliced open
2 slices	ripe tomato
2 thin slices	red onion
1/4 cup	shredded iceberg lettuce

1. First prepare your mayo. Cube your butter in 1/2-inch pieces and pulse it in a food processor to let it come up to room temperature.

2. In a small pot over low heat, combine the honey and rosemary. You want to gently warm the mixture for 3 to 4 minutes. When the honey has been infused, pour it into the food processor with the butter. Make sure to get all the honey out of the pot with a spatula.

3. Process the honey and butter together for 1 to 2 minutes until it's well combined.

4. Add the mayo, Tabasco, and salt to the processor and mix to combine. This will make more sauce than you need, but you can use it on all of your sandwiches and start eating more hamburgers.

5. Preheat your barbecue on high, and make sure it's as hot as you can get it.

6. Season your burgers with salt and pepper, place on the barbecue, and close the lid. Depending on the heat of your barbecue and how you like your meat cooked, it will take between 2 and 4 minutes per side to cook.

7. Once your burger has been flipped, put your sliced hamburger buns, cut sides down, on the top rack of the barbecue and close the lid.

8. After 30 seconds, your buns should be toasty and ready to be dressed any way you like.

9. Remove the burgers from the grill and let them rest for a minute or so while you dress the buns. Spread a healthy serving of the rosemary honey butter mayo on the buns, add ketchup or mustard if you like, and place the burgers on the bottom buns. Dress with tomato, onion, and lettuce, close them up, and enjoy.

[MADAME BOEUF]

NOTE: For the ground beef chuck, I like a blend of chuck, brisket, and hanger steak with a super-high fat content. You can ask a butcher to grind the meat up for you, or grind it yourself if you have a meat grinder at home. Use equal parts of the three different cuts to form patties.

LE CHEESEBURGER

I CAN PINPOINT THE MOMENT when I tried ham and cheese for the first time. My family and I had stopped at Tanglewood for a symphony and a picnic, and somehow this sandwich was handed to me. My Jewish mind basically exploded. Ham and cheese. I had always heard of such things, but only in fairy tales. I like to think that ham and cheese sandwiches were soon followed by cheeseburgers.

2 (5 oz)	beef patties (see note on page 189)
	Kosher salt and freshly ground black pepper
2 (3-inch)	classic hamburger buns, sliced open
2 (1 oz)	slices Canadian orange cheddar

1. Follow the directions to make Le Hamburger (page 189). As soon as you take your buns off the grill to dress them, add the cheddar cheese to your burgers and close the lid of the barbecue. After 30 or 40 seconds, your cheese should be perfectly melted onto your burgers. Proceed to dress and eat.

LE CHILI BURGER

THE CHILI WE MAKE IS CLASSIC COMPETITION-STYLE chili as per the International
Chili Society's rules and regulations, as below:

> "True chili is defined by the International Chili Society as any
> kind of meat, or combination of meats, cooked with chili peppers,
> various other spices, and other ingredients with the exception of
> items such as beans or spaghetti which are strictly forbidden."

There you have it. Pretty simple and self-explanatory. I love following this
recipe, but you can also choose to use a whole chuck roast cut into cubes
instead of the ground beef. It looks a little funny on a hot dog or burger,
but it's divine.

2 (5 oz)	beef patties (see note on page 189)
	Kosher salt and freshly ground black pepper
2 (3-inch)	classic hamburger buns, sliced open

CHILI:

	Vegetable oil, for frying
1 lb	ground beef
1	small Spanish onion, very finely diced
2 cloves	garlic, very finely chopped
2 tsp	ground cumin
1 tsp	ground fennel
3 Tbsp	mustard powder
2 Tbsp	smoked paprika
1 Tbsp	onion powder
1 Tbsp	garlic powder
1/2 tsp	chili flakes
1/4 tsp	ground cloves
2 Tbsp	tomato paste
2 tsp	kosher salt
2 tsp	freshly ground black pepper
3 Tbsp	maple syrup
2 Tbsp	apple cider vinegar + more to taste

1. First make the chili—you can do this
   the night before, and it will taste
   even better the next day. Heat a
   large pot or Dutch oven with a
   tight-fitting lid on medium heat,
   then add 2 Tbsp vegetable oil. Fry
   your ground beef in the oil,
   breaking up the beef as much as
   possible. Cook the meat until
   browned, then transfer the beef into
   a colander to drain all excess fat.

2. Return the pot to the heat, add
   another 2 Tbsp vegetable oil, and
   gently sweat out the onions and
   garlic until soft, about 2 to 3
   minutes. Then add the cumin, fennel,
   mustard powder, paprika, onion
   powder, garlic powder, chili flakes,
   and cloves, and toast them in the
   pot until very fragrant, about
   1 minute. Add the tomato paste and
   keep frying until it starts to look
   dry, about 3 to 4 minutes.

3. Add the ground beef back to the pot
   along with the salt, pepper, 2 cups
   water, and the maple syrup. Keep
   stirring the mix until the pot is
   fully deglazed. Turn the heat down
   to medium-low and put a lid on it.
   Cook this to a good consistency for
   about 1 hour, then taste for
   seasoning. Adjust with maple syrup
   and apple cider vinegar to your
   taste.

4. If making this chili ahead of time,
   cool overnight in the fridge, then
   reheat 1/2 cup chili per burger when
   you're ready.

5. Follow the directions to make
   Le Hamburger (page 189). When your
   burgers are ready, pour the chili
   right on top of the burgers and
   close them up in the buns.

NOTE: Simmering the spices over time
is what makes the chili thick and
delicious. You can also add crushed-up
tortilla or potato chips to thicken it
and add a different dimension.

[MADAME BOEUF]

LE BANQUET BURGER

WHILE THE ORIGINATOR OF THE BANQUET BURGER, a simple but genius concoction of a hamburger with cheese and bacon, is uncertain, I think it came from Fran's Restaurant in Toronto. It should also be noted that a small percentage of my body fat is made up from said banquet burger(s), french fries, onion rings, bacon, and milkshakes, remnants of my time there as a youngster.

4 slices	double-smoked bacon
2 (5 oz)	beef patties (see note on page 189)
	Kosher salt and freshly ground black pepper
2 (3-inch)	classic hamburger buns, sliced open
2 (1 oz)	slices Canadian orange cheddar

1. Follow the directions to make Le Hamburger (page 189), but before you put the burgers on the grill, you need to parcook your bacon. You want to do this ahead of time so you can render out as much fat as possible and avoid any flare-ups on the grill. To parcook the bacon, place it in a pan on medium heat and cook until most of the fat has rendered. Alternatively, you can cook it on a baking sheet in a 350°F oven for about 15 minutes.

2. Once you put your burgers on the grill, find a cooler spot on the grill to finish cooking your bacon. Keep an eye on it, as it can burn very easily, but you can cook this to be as crispy as you like. We usually cook it for 1 minute per side, but you can cook it a couple of minutes longer if you want.

3. Once the burgers are almost cooked, place the slices of cheese on top, followed by the crispy bacon. Close the lid of the barbecue for about 30 to 40 seconds, then remove the burgers once the cheese has melted. Proceed to dress and eat.

[MADAME BOEUF]

LE MADAME BOEUF BURGER

MY UNCLE IRV HAD A BABY-BLUE 1976 CADILLAC, and he once drove me to see Rae Dawn Chong in maybe one of her greatest performances as Ika in Quest for Fire. It was incredible to sit on my uncle's lap to drive as a 10-year-old, but even that experience was eclipsed by another part of our outing that day: when bacon crossed my lips for the first time. For a Jewish kid, it's hard to overstate the impact. I remember my uncle ordering bacon with his eggs, and my mind secretly exploded. I, of course, very nonchalantly did the same thing, and life was never the same. This burger is an ode to that breakfast, baby-blue Cadillacs, Rae Dawn Chong, hot dogs, and the blessed broken egg yolk.

4 slices	double-smoked bacon
2 (5 oz)	beef patties (see note on page 189)
	Kosher salt and freshly ground black pepper
2	kosher hot dogs, split in half lengthwise
1 Tbsp	unsalted butter
2	large eggs
2 (1 oz)	slices Canadian orange cheddar
2 (3-inch)	classic hamburger buns, sliced open

1. Follow the directions to make Le Hamburger (page 189), but before you put the burgers on the grill, you need to parcook your bacon. You want to do this ahead of time so you can render out as much fat as possible and avoid any flare-ups on the grill. To parcook the bacon, place it in a pan on medium heat and cook until most of the fat has rendered. Alternatively, you can cook it on a baking sheet in a 350°F oven for about 15 minutes.

2. Once you put your burgers on the grill, find a cooler spot on the grill to finish cooking your bacon. Keep an eye on it, as it can burn very easily, but you can cook this to be as crispy as you like. We usually cook it for 2 to 3 minutes.

3. Grill the split hot dogs until crispy and bubbly on each side, about 3 minutes per side.

4. Place a nonstick frying pan on the grill and add a little butter. Once the butter is hot, fry the egg over easy, about 45 seconds per side.

5. Once the burgers are almost cooked, place the slices of cheese on top, followed by the crispy bacon and the kosher hot-dog halves. Close the lid of the barbecue for about 30 to 40 seconds, then remove the burger once the cheese has melted. Place one egg on top of each burger, proceed to dress, close the buns, and eat.

MADAME BOEUF
AND FLEA
(Ye menu)

BURGERS	SIDES
Lettuce ONION MAYO	SHRIMP
HAMBURGER	COCKTAIL
CHEESEBURGER	HAND CUT FRIES
BANQUET BURGER	CHEESE FRIES
Grilled EGGPLANT	WHOLE PICKLE
MADAME BOEUF BURGER	EZELL'S SWEET
	SUMMER SLAW

ICE CREAM

ED'S REAL SCOOP
A SCOOP
TAHITIAN VANILLA, CHOCOLATE
BURNT MARSHMALLOW

ICE CREAM FLOA
ICE CREAM SLU

SHRIMP COCKTAIL

THESE SHRIMP BABIES come from Quebec and the St. Lawrence River. They're soft and sweet and little and delicious. I always try to sell them simply piled in a half avocado and dressed with Thousand Island dressing. It's reminiscent of old-school San Francisco dining. I try so many times, but no one ever buys it. I will keep trying. In the meantime, though, here's another good way to eat these.

2 lb	Matane shrimp
2 cups	shredded iceberg or romaine lettuce
1	lemon, cut into 6 wedges
1 cup	cocktail sauce (page 255)

1. Matane shrimp usually come cooked and frozen. Let them thaw in your fridge overnight. The next day, place them on a clean, dry dish towel, gather up all the edges, and firmly squeeze out any excess water. Let the shrimp dry on a separate clean, dry dish towel.

2. Once your shrimp are ready to go, serve them on a bed of shredded lettuce and garnish with lemon wedges and a side of cocktail sauce.

[MADAME BOEUF]

CHEESE FRIES

I CAME TO LOVE NACHO CHEESE MUCH LATER IN LIFE. When I was growing up, spray cheese in a can was more my thing, especially on Ritz crackers, or Triscuits, or a straight shot in the mouth. Now, though, as a grown-ass man, I know that nacho cheese is a far superior choice. This recipe is excellent company for nights alone on the couch, binge-watching absolutely anything.

FRIES
4 lb	russet potatoes
	Vegetable oil, for deep frying
	Kosher salt

CHEESE SAUCE:
2 cups	whole milk
1 Tbsp	sodium citrate (see note)
1 Tbsp	sambal oelek
4 cups	shredded orange cheddar, well packed

1. For the fries, cut your potatoes into strips that resemble french fries-not too small but not too big. You can do this on a mandoline or by hand, just make sure to cut them in evenly sized pieces so they cook all together. Soak the potatoes for about 30 minutes in lots of cold water to remove the starch. Change the water 4 times during this 30 minutes. Ideally, you would soak the potatoes overnight in the fridge and in twice as much water to pull out the extra starch. But if you gotta eat, you gotta eat.

2. When you're ready to fry, prepare your deep fryer or a large Dutch oven. Bring the oil temperature to 275°F. A kitchen thermometer is useful here, and make sure to use enough oil so that the potatoes can move around freely.

3. Drain your fries of all the water before you begin to fry. Make sure they're as dry as possible. Transfer the fries to the oil and blanch for 5 minutes. They should be soft but not golden brown. Line a large plate with paper towel, and, using a slotted spoon, transfer the fries to the prepared plate to soak up any excess oil. Cool the fries in the fridge, and turn your fryer up to 365°F.

4. While the oil heats up, prepare your cheese sauce. In a large pot, combine the milk, sodium citrate, and sambal oelek. Bring to a boil, then turn down to a simmer. Add your cheese to the pot and whisk constantly until smooth. This should take 2 to 3 minutes. Keep your sauce on low heat, as it can burn quite easily. If you're making the cheese sauce ahead of time, take the sauce off the heat at this step, cool, and reheat it in the microwave later.

5. Once the oil has reached temperature, transfer your fries back to the fryer and cook for 4 minutes or until golden brown and crispy. Line your large plate with fresh paper towel and, using a slotted spoon, transfer the finished fries to the plate to soak up any excess oil. Season immediately with kosher salt to taste.

6. To serve, place the fries on a clean platter and spoon the cheese sauce directly overtop.

NOTE: You can order sodium citrate online or buy it at a specialty kitchen store, but if you just can't find this, don't worry about it. Use cream instead of milk and it will be a little thicker regardless. In terms of garnishes, you can go crazy here. Chili? Fried egg? Scallions? Sour cream? Or all of the above? Your choice.

[MADAME BOEUF]

I DO NOT GIVE A RECIPE FOR POUTINE IN THIS BOOK. *C'est la vie, ma chérie.*

Ezell's Sweet Summer Slaw

Potato Salad.

EZELL'S SWEET SUMMER SLAW

SERVES 5

STORY GOES SOMETHING LIKE THIS: I had a cook who worked for a fish camp in Alabama, and he stole this recipe from the very, very sweet old lady who owned and ran the joint. She would make the slaw in the back so nobody would steal the recipe. I apologize to this woman, and thank her for making my life so much richer with her coleslaw.

1/2 head	green cabbage, thinly sliced
1 Tbsp	kosher salt
1/2	red onion, grated on a box grater
1 cup	sweet relish
4 Tbsp	white sugar
3/4 cup	mayo

1. In a large bowl, mix your cabbage with the salt and let it sit overnight in the fridge to develop the flavors, or for less time for crisp, fresh goodness.

2. When you're ready to proceed, squeeze all the water out of the cabbage and transfer it to a fresh bowl.

3. Add the grated onions, relish, sugar, and mayo to the cabbage and mix to combine. Let sit for an hour or two before serving. This is best served the first day you make it, but it's still pretty darn good the second day.

POTATO SALAD

I HAVE NEVER BEEN MUCH OF A POTATO SALAD GUY, but I played around in the 90s with warm potato salad. Lots of bacon and mustard and grilled dandelion greens. It worked for me, but a few years back, we needed something cold and scoopable for Big Crow. The addition of hard-boiled eggs, pickles, and al dente potatoes made me very happy and still keeps me smiling. This salad was a huge hit at Big Crow, so it was an easy and delicious addition for the beautiful customers of Madame Boeuf.

3 lb	Yukon Gold potatoes
	Kosher salt and freshly ground black pepper
1 1/2 cups	ranch dressing (page 253)
3/4 cup	diced full-sour pickles
7	scallions, thinly sliced
1/4	red onion, diced small
3	large hard-boiled eggs, roughly chopped

1. Cut the potatoes, skin on, into 1 1/2-inch cubes, then put them in a pot with 1 Tbsp kosher salt. Cover with water.

2. Bring the potatoes up to a simmer over medium-high heat, and cook until they're quite tender, about 30 to 45 minutes. Strain the potatoes.

3. While the potatoes are still hot, transfer them to a large bowl and mix with the ranch dressing, pickles, scallions, red onions, and eggs. Taste for seasoning and adjust with salt and pepper if necessary.

4. Refrigerate for a couple of hours before serving.

[MADAME BOEUF]

SALE

THE ULTIMATE BAKE SALE is always at my mom's house at the breaking of the fast for Yom Kippur. Everyone brings a dish for the meal, and the dessert table turns into a dream of goodness. I wish there were more bake sales in my life. I think communities should get together and have them once a month. It's a shame, really— all these home cooks make something delicious or even junky-delicious, only to be sold to kids at school? It's crazy. I have brought the bake sale back to the adult masses at Madame Boeuf.

CHALLAH STICKY BUNS

	Challah dough (page 65)
1 cup	unsalted butter, room temperature, + extra for greasing
1 1/2 cups	brown sugar
1 Tbsp	kosher salt
2 Tbsp	ground cinnamon
2 cups	brown-butter caramel sauce (page 26)
1 cup	raisins

1. Get your challah dough ready to the point when it's had its first proof (through step 5 on pages 65-66), then preheat your oven to 350°F.

2. On a lightly floured surface, punch down your dough and roll it out into a large rectangle, about 16 x 24 inches. It should be about 1/2 inch thick.

3. Without touching the top 2 inches of dough, evenly smear the butter all over the rest of the dough's surface. Cover this same area with the brown sugar, salt, and cinnamon.

4. Roll the dough away from you, making sure that it's nice and even. The last bit of exposed dough is what seals your roll together.

5. Grease a 9- x 13-inch baking pan with butter and line it with parchment paper, then pour in the caramel sauce and raisins, making sure that they're evenly spread around.

6. Cut your roll into 15 pieces, then place them spiral side down in the caramel sauce. Cover with a clean dish towel and let the buns sit for 20 minutes on top of your stove to get one last proof. Remove the dish towel.

7. Place the baking pan in the oven and bake for 25 to 30 minutes.

8. Remove the buns from the oven and let them rest for 10 minutes before serving. Use a small spatula or a large serving spoon to lift out the buns.

NANAIMO BARS

BASE:

1/2 cup	unsalted butter
1/4 cup	white sugar
1/3 cup	cocoa powder
1	large egg, beaten
2 cups	graham cracker crumbs
1 1/4 cups	shredded coconut
1/2 tsp	kosher salt

CREAMY MIDDLE:

1 cup	unsalted butter
6 Tbsp	whole milk
2 Tbsp	custard powder
1/4 tsp	kosher salt
4 cups	icing sugar

CHOCOLATE TOPPING:

1 cup	dark chocolate chips
6 Tbsp	heavy cream (35%)

1. For the base, first prepare a double boiler on your stove: Fill a large pot about a quarter full of water and bring to a boil. Reduce the heat to a simmer and place a heatproof bowl overtop. Make sure the bottom of the bowl is not touching the water.

2. In the double boiler, melt the butter, sugar, and cocoa powder, mixing regularly until smooth. Add the egg, stirring constantly until the mixture has just started to thicken a bit, about 1 to 2 minutes.

3. Remove the bowl from the heat and stir in the graham cracker crumbs, coconut, and salt.

4. Line a 9- x 13-inch baking pan with parchment paper. Spoon the graham cracker mixture inside, press it down firmly and evenly, and refrigerate until solid, about 2 hours.

5. For the creamy middle layer, in a stand mixer with the paddle attachment, whip the butter until light and airy, about 2 minutes on medium speed.

6. Add the milk, custard powder, salt, and icing sugar and mix on low speed until all the ingredients have been incorporated. Increase the speed to medium and whip until light and fluffy, about 5 minutes. Pour this creamy mix onto your solid base, make sure it's evenly spread out, and refrigerate for about 2 hours.

7. For the chocolate topping, melt the chocolate and cream together in a double boiler over low heat, stirring constantly. When the chocolate has melted, remove from the heat and let rest for about 5 to 10 minutes. You want the temperature to come down but still keep the chocolate completely melted. Pour this over the cream layer and, using a rubber spatula, spread it out evenly. Chill in the fridge for at least 3 hours before serving.

[MADAME BOEUF]

BAKERMAN BARS

BASE:
1 cup	unsalted butter, melted
4 cups	graham cracker crumbs
1/2 tsp	kosher salt

TOPPING:
2 cups	shredded coconut, divided
1 2/3 cups	chocolate chips
2 cups	pecan halves
1/2 tsp	kosher salt
2 (14 oz) cans	sweetened condensed milk

1. Preheat your oven to 325°F.

2. For the base, in a large bowl, mix the butter, graham cracker crumbs, and salt. Transfer the mixture to a 9- x 13-inch baking pan and spread it out evenly. Pack the base down tightly!

3. For the topping, evenly spread 1/2 cup coconut over the base. Follow with all of the chocolate chips, pecans, and salt. Finish by sprinkling the remainder of the coconut overtop.

4. Slowly and evenly, pour the two cans of condensed milk all over, making sure you get every last drop out.

5. Bake for 20 minutes in the preheated oven, then rotate the dish and bake for another 15 to 20 minutes until the top is golden and bubbling.

6. Let cool fully before slicing into 12 bars and serving.

[MADAME BOEUF]

BROWNIES

3 1/4 cups	dark chocolate chips, divided
1 3/4 cups	unsalted butter + extra for greasing
6	large eggs
4 tsp	vanilla paste or extract
2 3/4	cups brown sugar
1 1/3	cups all-purpose flour
1 Tbsp	baking powder
2 tsp	kosher salt
1 cup	white chocolate chips

1. Preheat the oven to 300°F.

2. Prepare a double boiler on your stove (see page 207).

3. In the double boiler, melt half of the dark chocolate chips and the butter. Once the chocolate has melted, remove the bowl from the heat and set aside at room temperature.

4. In a stand mixer, cream together the eggs, vanilla, and brown sugar until light and fluffy, about 5 minutes.

5. In a large bowl, sift together the flour, baking powder, and salt. Then fold the creamed sugar mixture into the dry ingredients. Be careful not to overmix.

6. Fold in the melted chocolate and butter mixture.

7. Fold in the white chocolate chips and remaining dark chocolate chips.

8. Grease a 9- x 13-inch baking pan with butter and line it with parchment paper.

9. Pour in the brownie batter and bake for about 1 hour in the preheated oven. When it's done, a toothpick inserted into the center should come out clean . . . but undercooked brownies are also delicious.

TRIPS AND OTHER ADVENTURES

Temaga hi
Shore lunch —

AS WE APPROACH THE END OF THIS BOOK, I don't want to leave you with the impression that all we did when writing it was throw parties and eat too much. No. Sometimes we went on holiday, too. For both Anthony and me, inspiration is often found on the road, and throughout the 18 months or so that we worked on this project together we got out as often as we could. I never once saw Anthony in a bad mood, but I also never saw him happier than when he was outside somewhere, regardless of the weather, cooking over an open fire. To not include some stories from those experiences would not give a full picture of who Anthony is as a chef. That elemental connection to cooking food clearly inspires him and I think that unalloyed love of simplicity, nature, and freedom is apparent in aspects of all his restaurants.

WE'RE SOMEWHERE IN THE MIDDLE OF OBABIKA LAKE (an Ojibwe word meaning "one lake that is almost two"), about 300 miles north of Toronto in the vast and wild Temagami region. Anthony's showing off his J-stroke, an advanced canoeing paddle honed over years of Ontario summer camp as a kid, and we're on our way to a sacred place.

Yesterday, our little group drove up as far as the road would take us, then piled into a floatplane for the final push to the lake. Here we met the rugged and magnificently named Constantin Von Flotow of the luxury wilderness-camping outfitters Outpost Co. Constantin, in collaboration with the local custodian of the lake, had sought out an especially beautiful and well-situated spit of land and built a camp that would make a voyageur proud. A real teepee and a few canvas tents, outfitted with big, comfortable beds and carpets set on raised wooden floors, were set up at the tree line.

There was no electricity or running water (or cell service), but that hadn't stopped camp chef Charlotte Langley from laying out an incredible feast: fresh oysters by the dozen, hot- and cold-smoked salmon, tomatoes with burrata, her own tins of mussels in tomato oil, fresh sausages, and warm bread. And some impossibly cold Champagne, just to welcome us.

After lunch, a few people retired to their tent for a nap, others hiked up to a river mouth nearby, some went for a swim. The day slid by easily. A picnic table was moved out from under a tarp and closer to the shore to take advantage of the sunset that perfectly coincided with the moonrise just in time for dinner.

We were about halfway through a huge pot of shakshouka (the spicy Israeli/ Tunisian tomato dish) and had hardly put a dent in all of the bannock and fire-roasted chickens when a trio of canoes paddled into view from around the cove. It was a group of campers from an all-girls camp a few lakes over. They were on a two-week portage trip, exhausted, lost, and filthy.

Constantin sorted them out with directions and pointed out a good spot to set up camp on a little island nearby, and the girls paddled away. Anthony and Rob, who grew up doing this kind of thing and whose own kids are now having these same kinds of adventures, packed up all the leftover food, loaded it in a canoe, and paddled it over to their camp. We could hear the cheers of joy from across the water when they discovered what was in store for them.

The campers stopped by the next morning, looking considerably happier but only marginally less dirty, to say thank you and rave about the food. We wished them good luck and waved until they disappeared around the bend.

Charlotte had been up early, putting together what she called her "truck-stop breakfast": pancakes with good maple syrup, bloody steaks, rashers of bacon, a cast-iron pan full of fried eggs, and a salad bowl's worth of fresh berries. "Eat up," Constantin said. "We're going to need our energy for the paddle up to the Conjuring Rock." And now here we are, paddling and reaching peak Canadiana. Everything is quiet except for the sound of our paddles splashing gently against the water. The stillness is broken by the call of a loon, its haunting cry reverberating among the old-growth pines, and the sound of a beer cracking open.

We continue to paddle along in silence, the canoes slowly drifting closer together and then further away from each other in the calm water. A few hours later, we pull up to a sandy beach, secure the boats with ropes to the trees, and hike our way over to Chee-skon Lake.

It's a sunny day, but the way the granite cliffs and old-growth pines press up against the lake, the whole place appears in shadow. Something about the light and the stillness and the landscape really does imbue the lake with a strong feeling of spirituality.

"The Anishinaabe have been coming here to fast and heal and seek guidance for centuries," Constantin explains. "This is a very sacred place." Conjuring Rock, a slender limestone tower that has sheared away from the surrounding cliff face, is what drew them here. "People came to communicate with the spirit world," Constantin says. "There used to be three rocks like this, but now only this one remains. I've spent the night here before and there is definitely a powerful energy."

People slowly drift off on their own to sit and contemplate the clear water and study the Conjuring Rock before gathering again a little while later for the hike back to the boats. Pulling away from the shoreline, we are plunged into warm, full sun. Constantin guides us to a landing spot where we haul out and carry lunch up to a bright promontory.

Lunch is contained in two big wanigans, wooden crates designed to carry food on canoe trips. Wanigan is a borrowed Algonquian word roughly meaning "a chest for supplies," and it's an ingenious contraption. Watertight and made to float, it's carried by means of a strap that goes over the forehead so the box rests on the carrier's back. "Even in these days of PU-coated nylon backpacks and insulated packing cooler cubes, you can't beat a good old wanigan," Rob says, hauling one up a steep cliff.

Despite the process looking a bit dangerous, they must be easy to carry because ours are extremely full. Anthony wants to prepare a shore lunch and he hasn't left an ingredient behind. Soon we've got a little fire going. There are cans of beans heating up in the coals, potato hash, and roasted onions cooking in aluminum foil pouches. Fresh lake fish, for which Charlotte has provided us with tins of tartar sauce, get dredged and fried in cast-iron pans over the flames.

So far, so standard (if unusually delicious) for a camping shore lunch. Then
Anthony pulls out some whole lobes of foie gras. "I just thought we should
have these," he says. They get laid into a blistering-hot skillet right over
the fire and immediately start to sear. When they achieve exactly the dark,
caramelized crust he wants, he douses them with a generous pour of whisky to
cool down the pan and pull together a sauce. Soon we're all dipping foie gras-
loaded bread into the pan as our simple shore lunch goes from merely
incredible to utterly unforgettable.

Back at camp that evening around dusk, as Anthony builds a fire on the beach
and everyone relaxes with their drink of choice, the sound of an outboard
motor in the distance breaks the silence. A lone figure, upright in the stern,
pilots a little aluminum fishing boat right toward us.

"That must be Grant," Constantin says.

Grant is the only person from the Temagami First Nation who still lives on
this, their territorial land. He pulls the boat in to the shore and steps out
wearing a buckskin coat. He pulls an elaborate feathered headdress out of the
hull and carries a tall walking stick covered in carved snakes and bears that
seem to grow organically out of natural knots in the wood.

Introductions are made and we ask him if he'll tell us a bit about what it's
like to live in such a remote and beautiful place.

"I've lived here my whole life," he says. "To me, the whole land is sacred,
not just a plant here or a tree there. Nature provides me with everything
I need. When you start living with nature, you learn from her as well.
I'm still learning. I'm learning the animals' habits and to take what I can
use and leave the rest for next year or the year after. I walk every day on
this soil that machinery never destroyed. It's such a great feeling."

"Does it ever get lonely?" I ask.

"I never feel alone," he says, "because there's always birds chirping and
squirrels calling. They're my neighbors. I can't communicate with them, but
they're my neighbors."

"Who's going to look after this land after you're gone?" Anthony asks.

"I'm not going," he says.

TEMAGAMI CAMPING SHORE LUNCH

I GREW UP GOING TO ALGONQUIN PARK and camping in what I thought was the most glorious nature of all time. Then I found Temagami, which is my new most-glorious-nature-of-all-time spot. There's nothing better than seeing the sun set and the full moon rise at the same time. Nothing grander than washing your lover's body in the early morning mist in a pristine lake. Nothing sweeter than eating and drinking with great friends as the loons call. Nothing more rewarding than hiking and canoeing along the routes of the ancestors of this land, seeing pictographs and some of the oldest red and white pine trees in Ontario. On my camping trips, I like to cook a shore lunch, which is the epitome of Canadian cuisine. Most people would pack a shore lunch that is pretty bare bones, but I'm not most people. Please allow me to present the best shore lunch in the world, as voted by me, beginning with the most essential dish, foie gras. I've written this recipe so you can make it at home, but the fireside chef's instructions are just as simple. Heat a cast-iron pan over the coals of the fire. Sear the whole foie gras hard on all sides. Flambé with Canadian rye whisky and serve ASAP.

1	whole lobe grade A foie gras (about 1 lb)
1 Tbsp	duck salt (page 250)
2 oz	Lot No. 40 whisky or whatever your favorite is
1	large Spanish onion, thinly sliced
1 loaf	good-quality sourdough bread, for serving

1. Season your foie with the duck salt and let it sit for 30 minutes.

2. Transfer the foie to a resealable plastic bag along with the whisky, and refrigerate overnight. Give this a bit of a mix a few times to make sure it's marinating evenly.

3. The next day, line a roasting pan with parchment paper and put the sliced onions right in the center of the pan. Put the foie gras on top of the onions and try to make sure that the onions are all neatly tucked under the foie. Pour any excess whisky from the marinade bag over the foie to soak into the onions.

4. Preheat the oven to 400°F while you wait for the foie to come to room temperature. Don't cook it when it's still ice-cold.

5. Roast the foie in the oven for 12 to 15 minutes. When it's ready, it should be caramelized on the outside and have a jelly-like texture.

6. Serve the foie gras and onions next to each other on a platter with a loaf of good sourdough.

IF, LIKE MY EDITOR, you think that foie gras is a strange choice for a camping trip, I will now give you the recipe for the rest of the shore lunch, which my editor may or may not be happy with. This is rugged cooking, so don't sweat the small stuff. Dirt will get absolutely everywhere, including in your mouth.

WHAT YOU WILL NEED BEFORE YOU COOK:		FOOD YOU WILL NEED:	
	Canoe, paddles, and life jackets	2	(2 lb) freshly caught whole fish
	Sunscreen and hats if it's hot	1 can	creamed corn
		1 can	Heinz baked beans
	Patience and lots of water to drink	1 lb	unsalted butter
	Fishing rods and bait		Vegetable oil, for frying fish
	2 good cast-iron pans	2 cups	buttermilk, for dredging fish
1	fillet knife		
	Plates and sporks	4 cups	Original Shore Lunch Breading Mix or other breadcrumbs
1	can opener		
	Garbage bags		
	Towels	4	Yukon Gold potatoes, boiled until perfect and cut into cubes
1	metal or glass bottle with a tight-fitting lid to bring oil in and out with you		
		6 slices	bacon, diced
		1	yellow onion, thinly sliced
			Kosher salt and freshly ground black pepper in a vial, premixed at home
			Tabasco
		1 loaf	good bread
		1	lemon, sliced into wedges
		1 flask	filled with Canadian whisky

Fried Perch
Hash - Back Phat
Baked Beans
Sweet Corn Toast - 1000 island Dressing

Foie gras
Tartar Sauce

1. Go fishing in a great lake and catch a couple of fish about 2 lb each. Make sure you release the little guys back into the wild.

2. Find a good place on the shore and build a raging fire. Let the fire turn to embers, but keep feeding the fire. While you wait for the fire to be ready, fillet your fish.

3. Nestle the cans of creamed corn and baked beans around the fire, almost in the embers, to get hot.

4. Set one of your cast-iron pans on the embers, with 3 Tbsp of butter and 3 Tbsp of oil inside, to get hot.

5. While the pan heats up, soak the fish fillets in the buttermilk for 5 minutes. Then dredge the fillets in the Shore Lunch Breading Mix.

6. Place the fillets in the hot pan and fry the fish in the oil-butter mixture for about 3 minutes per side. Transfer the fish to a plate and pour the oil into the metal or glass bottle you brought just for this purpose.

7. Put the pan, with more oil and butter, back on the embers to get hot.

8. When the pan is hot, cook the potatoes, bacon, and onions together until crisp, or until you can't wait any longer because your back is killing you from squatting and bending over the fire.

9. Season the potato mixture with salt, pepper, Tabasco to taste, and a little dirt and ash you didn't see.

10. Carefully remove the beans and corn from the embers and open them with the can opener.

11. Slice or tear the bread into chunks, get grease on it like the oil or butter, and toast it a bit or just get it warm or just start eating it fresh.

12. Place a piece of fish and some beans, corn, and potato mixture on a plate, with a bit of lemon for the fish. Eat away. Drink some whisky. You'll be dirty.

13. Put out your fire, clean up, and bring all the garbage with you. Always leave a campsite as clean as you found it, and if it wasn't clean when you got there, make it clean before you leave.

HOUSE

PARTY

WE'VE BEEN FORTUNATE ENOUGH to have worked closely with the music industry in
Toronto for many years. We've catered dinners and a show with the band Do Make
Say Think and have headlined backstage artist hospitality at festivals like Field
Trip, WayHome, and Boots and Hearts. Arts & Crafts is a local music label, and
I wanted to throw them a party at my house before their big Field Trip music
festival. First on my menu was a butter bar. Few things are better in life than
poached shellfish with a butter bathtub to dip it all in. Variety is king here:
lobster, shrimp, octopus, and mussels and clams to round it all out. Picking your
fishmonger is super-important too—in Toronto, I always buy my fish from Hooked in
Kensington Market or Diana's in Scarborough.

BUTTER BAR

SEAFOOD:

2 (1 lb)	lobsters
	Kosher salt
2 lb	shrimp, peeled and deveined
1 (2 lb)	octopus, beak removed

COURT BOUILLON:

1/2 head	fennel, roughly chopped
1/2 head	celery, roughly chopped
1	white onion, roughly chopped
4	bay leaves
1	lemon, halved
1 cup	white wine
2 Tbsp	kosher salt
1 Tbsp	black peppercorns

MUSSELS AND CLAMS:

1/2 cup	unsalted butter, divided
2	shallots, thinly sliced, divided
4 cloves	garlic, thinly sliced, divided
2 tsp	chili flakes, divided
3 lb	littleneck clams, cleaned
2 lb	mussels, cleaned and beards removed
2 cups	white wine, divided
2 tsp	kosher salt, divided

BUTTER BATH:

1 lb	unsalted butter
1 lb	ramps or scallions, cleaned and cut into small pieces
1/2 Tbsp	freshly ground black pepper, or more to taste
	Lemon wedges, for serving
	Cocktail skewers, for serving

1. You'll want to cook your seafood a day ahead of time or first thing in the morning to give it a chance to cool thoroughly.

2. Make sure your lobsters are frisky; this means that they're as fresh as possible. Bring a large pot of salted water to a boil—you should use about 4 quarts water and 4 Tbsp kosher salt. Boil the lobsters for about 7 to 8 minutes each. Remove them from the water, transfer to a large bowl, and cool in the fridge. Don't cool them in water or in an ice-water bath. Once cold, crack the lobsters, remove all the meat from the tail, claws, and legs, and cut into chunks for serving.

3. To cook your shrimp and octopus, first make your court bouillon. In a large pot, combine the fennel, celery, onions, bay leaves, lemon halves, wine, salt, and peppercorns. Add 6 quarts water and bring up to a simmer for at least 30 minutes before using. Once the flavors have had a chance to infuse, drop the shrimp into the liquid and give them a quick stir. Let the shrimp cook for 1 1/2 to 2 minutes until they have all turned pink on the outside. With a slotted spoon, remove the shrimp from the bouillon (reserving the liquid for your octopus) and spread them out on a tray. Cool the shrimp in the fridge; once they're cool, keep them in a covered container until you're ready to serve.

4. Put the whole octopus into the court bouillon and simmer for 1 to 1 1/2 hours, until you can put a paring knife through one of the legs with medium resistance. Once cooked, remove the pot from the heat and let the octopus cool to room temperature in the liquid. Separate all of the legs with a knife and cut the legs into chunks for serving. You can remove the skin easily with your hands if you like.

5. For the clams, heat a large pan with a tight-fitting lid on medium-high. Place 1/4 cup butter in the pan and sauté one sliced shallot, two cloves sliced garlic, and 1 tsp chili flakes for 15 seconds. Once you see the butter start to turn a bit brown, add the clams, 1 cup wine, and 1 tsp salt. Stir quickly, then cover with the lid. Turn the heat down to medium and cook for 5 minutes. After 5 minutes, remove the lid and cook for another 3 minutes, picking out each clam as it opens. Discard any clams that don't open after 8 minutes of total cooking time, and reserve the cooking liquor inside the pan. Once the clams are cool, remove the meat and transfer it back into the liquor to stay juicy until you're ready to serve.

6. For the mussels, cook them exactly the same way as you did the clams, starting with the butter, shallot, garlic, and chili flakes. Add the mussels and remaining wine and salt. Stir and cover, but keep in mind that the mussels will be ready in 2 1/2 to 4 minutes. Remove each mussel as it opens, and discard any that don't open. Once cool, remove the meat and transfer it back to the cooking liquor until you're ready to serve.

7. To prepare the butter bath, place a small pot on medium-low heat. Add the butter and let it melt and simmer gently. Continually skim the foam with a spoon as it rises to the top, until the butter is clear and clarified. Once the butter is melted and warm, add the ramps and pepper and allow to hang out and infuse for 10 to 15 minutes before serving.

8. To assemble your butter bar, artfully arrange all the cooked shellfish in piles on a large silver platter. Transfer the butter to a bowl and place the bowl in the middle of the whole thing. Garnish with lemon wedges and lots of skewers all around to pick and dip the shellfish.

OYSTER BAR

TORONTO IS KING OF THE OYSTER BARS in Canada and maybe in the world. We have a long, storied history of east coasters settling in Toronto to open, shuck at, and serve at oyster bars. Adam Calhoun, the owner of Oyster Boy, is one of my favorites. This oyster bar is a perfect addition to a fancy music party.

MIGNONETTE:

1 1/2 cups	red wine vinegar
1/4 cup	white sugar
2 Tbsp	kosher salt
1 tsp	freshly ground black pepper
1 cup	finely chopped ramps, stems only (scallions can be used as a substitute)

Garnishes:

6	lemons
1 (4-inch)	piece fresh horseradish
1/2 cup	cocktail sauce (page 255)
36	fresh oysters, scrubbed

1. For the mignonette, in a medium pot over medium-high heat, bring the vinegar, sugar, salt, and pepper to a simmer. Once the liquid has come to a simmer, transfer it to a bowl, add the ramps, and cool in the fridge for at least 1 hour.

2. Cut each lemon into 6 wedges for squeezing (so you have a total of 36 pieces), and grate your horseradish at the very last second so it's as strong as possible. Place the lemons, horseradish, and cocktail sauce in their own small bowls.

3. For the oysters, if you don't have a lot of experience shucking, buy east coast oysters, as they're easier to open. But if you're more experienced, get adventurous. The world is your oyster! To shuck the oysters, fold a towel over itself several times, and hold the oyster in the middle of the towel. Wrap the towel around the oyster, leaving the hinge exposed. Place the blade of your oyster knife firmly against the opening of the hinge and rotate the blade to pop the oyster open. Don't push too hard, or you can hurt yourself and the oyster. Slide the blade underneath the meat to separate the oyster from the shell, then carefully make sure that there is no broken shell around the edges of the meat. Serve the oysters on ice to keep cold, and place the bowls of mignonette, lemons, grated horseradish, and cocktail sauce alongside.

CAVIAR BAR

ONE OF MY FAVORITE DISHES of all time is the caviar sandwich at Grand Central Oyster Bar in New York. I could eat there every day, and when I visit New York for even the shortest time, I always make the pilgrimage. Acadian Sturgeon and Caviar in New Brunswick makes some of the finest caviar I know. In addition to their impeccable eggs, we use their smoked sturgeon at Schmaltz. The textures are meaty with a good hint of smoke. This is just the right dish to round out your party.

BUCKWHEAT PANCAKES:

2 1/4 tsp	active dry yeast
1/2 cup	buckwheat flour
1/2 cup	all-purpose flour
1/2 tsp	kosher salt
3/4 cup	plain yogurt
1/2 Tbsp	unsalted butter, melted
2	eggs, separated
3/4 tsp	white sugar
1/2 cup	clarified butter or ghee, for frying
2	large hard-boiled eggs
3 Tbsp	finely chopped fresh chives
3 Tbsp	finely chopped shallots
1/4 cup	crème fraîche or sour cream
1 tin	(30 g/1 oz or 50 g/1 3/4 oz) caviar from Acadian Sturgeon and Caviar (available by mail order, or use a similar caviar)

1. To make the buckwheat pancakes, you'll need three separate bowls. In a small bowl, combine the yeast with 1/2 cup warm water. Let it bloom for 5 to 10 minutes.

2. In a medium-size bowl, sift together the buckwheat flour, all-purpose flour, and salt.

3. In a large bowl, combine the yogurt mixture, butter, egg yolks, and sugar.

4. Pour the flour mixture into the large bowl with the yogurt, keeping it to one side of the bowl, and pour the yeast mixture into the large bowl on the other side. Whisk to combine, but don't overmix. Cover with a clean dish towel and let it sit in a warm place for about 30 minutes to proof. When it's ready, it should look gassy and bigger than before.

5. Wipe your medium bowl clean of the flour and whisk the egg whites together until you get stiff peaks. If you aren't willing to hold the bowl upside down over your own head, the whites aren't ready.

6. When the whites are stiff and the batter has proofed, use a rubber spatula to very gently fold the whites into the batter. Mix until just combined, but don't overmix.

7. Preheat the oven to 175°F. Heat a large pan over medium heat, then add some clarified butter. Use a 1 Tbsp measure to scoop out each pancake from the batter, and fry only three to four pancakes at a time. You don't want them to burn or for the pan to cool off too much. The pancakes should take about 2 minutes per side. Put these on a baking sheet in the oven to stay warm until you're ready to eat, but try and eat them as soon as possible.

8. To assemble the caviar bar, cut your hard-boiled eggs in half and separate the yolks from the whites. Rinse your whites under water to remove any yolk left behind, then dry with a towel. Grate the whites through the fine side of a box grater or on a coarse rasp, then clean the tool and grate the yolks.

9. Find your mother's fanciest sterling-silver platter and arrange all the garnishes in a very fancy flower pattern. Or just place big mounds of garnish on the platter, which is also perfection. Place the caviar, tin and all, in the middle of the garnishes. Wrap the pancakes in a towel to keep them warm, and build and eat and build and eat.

COTTAGE COUNTRY COOKING

MY ZAIDY, SIMON GOTTLIEB, built our family cottage in the early 70s on what was once Crown land near Barrie, Ontario—one of the most spectacular cities in the world. Today it is an easy hour-long drive from Toronto. I have given up trips to Thailand, Mexico, and Iceland to spend more time at the cottage. I don't travel anywhere in the summer, as I don't want to give up my time in the pristine nature of the cottage and the beauty of Ontario. With all my family and friends here, it is my happiest of all happy places. My mom does most everything at the cottage, with cooking help from me, but she leads the charge. Craigy gets the firewood and shucks the oysters. Lorne makes the cobblers and Randi helps my mom. My dad opens the wine and pours the water. Bless him.

MIAMI RIBS

FOR ME, Miami ribs were a substitute for pork ribs on the barbecue at home (until I found pork ribs). As a Jew, I didn't eat ribs until much later in life. Well, that's not quite true, so let me clarify. As Jews and quasi-kosher people, we didn't eat pork at home . . . That's not true either. Let me clarify. Chinese food was the exception to our kosher laws growing up. We could eat wonton soup, ribs, and anything else, as long as it was Chinese food. All other pork foods from all other nationalities were still not kosher. In the absence of non-Chinese-food ribs, my cousin Howie introduced me to Miami ribs. He first made them for me at the cottage, and I have never looked back.

5 lb	Miami ribs
	Chinatown marinade, enough to cover the ribs (from the fried rice recipe on page 146)
1/4 cup	toasted sesame seeds

DILL CUCUMBERS:

3	English cucumbers, thinly sliced on a mandoline
3 Tbsp	white sugar
2 Tbsp	kosher salt
1 tsp	chili flakes
1/4 cup	apple cider vinegar
1/4 cup	chopped fresh dill
1/2 cup	thinly sliced red onions

1. Marinate the Miami ribs in the Chinatown marinade in the fridge overnight, or for 12 hours.

2. In a bowl, combine the cucumber slices, sugar, salt, chili flakes, vinegar, dill, and red onions, and mix and massage by hand. Cover the bowl with plastic wrap and refrigerate overnight, or for 12 hours.

3. Remove the Miami ribs from the marinade and place them on a large plate, reserving the liquid. Transfer the leftover marinade to a medium pot over medium heat, and reduce the marinade by half to make a sauce. Transfer the sauce to a bowl.

4. Preheat a barbecue on high. Bring the sauce and a grilling brush outside to the barbecue, along with the ribs.

5. Grill the ribs for about 2 to 3 minutes per side, brushing with extra sauce to make them nice and sticky.

6. Place the cooked ribs on a clean platter and sprinkle with the toasted sesame seeds.

7. Drain the cucumbers and serve in a bowl on the side.

CLAM CHOWDER

DEAR CLAM CHOWDER:

I am writing to tell you that I love you. From my early memories of Campbell's soup made with a little milk to thin you out, to versions I made as I became a cook and tried to gussy you up (which you didn't need at all), I have learned so much from you. I learned that you don't really need a thickener or roux, and that letting the vegetables gently break down will do the trick. That you love bacon but just some salt-cured back fat is the key. That Tabasco was invented just for you and that using it as a seasoning is the way to go. Tarragon and dill make you better and fresher and more delicious. A good chunk of dark rye with cold butter is your best accessory, along with a great glass of rosé. Thank you, Chowder, for everything you do and for listening to me all these years.

Yours,
AR

CLAMS:

1 lb	littleneck clams
1/4 cup	canola oil
1 cup	thinly sliced Spanish onions
1/2 cup	white wine

CHOWDER:

1/4 cup	canola oil
2 cups	medium-diced Spanish onions
1 cup	medium-diced carrots
1 cup	medium-diced celery
1/2 tsp	chili flakes
2 cups	medium-diced Yukon Gold potatoes
3 cups	heavy cream (35%)
2 Tbsp	chopped fresh tarragon + extra for garnish
6 dashes	Tabasco
1/4 cup	white wine
1 (2 lb)	lobster, cooked and meat removed (optional)

1. Rinse the clams thoroughly under cold water for 20 minutes to get rid of any sand. In a medium pot with a tight-fitting lid, heat the canola oil on high heat, then sauté the onions until they just start to turn translucent, about 1 minute. Add the clams, stir quickly, then add the wine. Cover the pot with the lid right away and turn the heat down to medium. Cook for 3 to 5 minutes, until the clams have opened. Discard any clams that haven't opened. Transfer the clams to a bowl and reserve the clam liquor for later.

2. For the chowder, in a large stockpot, heat the canola oil on medium heat, then add the onions, carrots, celery, and chili flakes and sweat them until the veg have become soft, about 3 to 4 minutes. Add the potatoes and keep stirring for another minute, then add the heavy cream and the reserved clam juices. Let the soup come up to a simmer. Continue to simmer until the potatoes are just cooked, about 20 minutes. Add the tarragon, Tabasco, white wine, and cooked clams to the pot. If you're using lobster as well, add it at this step.

3. Bring the soup up to temperature, spoon out and divide the veg evenly among your serving bowls, then top with the creamy broth. Garnish with the seafood and more picked tarragon.

ROB'S BREAD

MAKES 2 LOAVES

I CANNOT SAY ENOUGH ABOUT ROBERT WILDER, my partner in all of my endeavors and my BFF. Meeting Rob changed—and saved—my life. He has made my dreams come true and made me a better man along the way. I trust him with our business and have complete faith that he will lead us down the path of righteousness. I love him and his family and feel so fortunate that I'm a part of his life. Also, Rob makes good food.

BLOOM:

1 Tbsp	active dry yeast
1 Tbsp	sea salt
3 cups	lukewarm water

BREAD:

5 Tbsp	olive oil
1/2 cup	honey
6 2/3 cups	organic whole wheat flour, divided (we like Bob's Red Mill)
1/2 cup	sesame, sunflower, pumpkin, or poppy seeds, or even raisins if you like (optional)

1. In a bowl, mix the yeast, sea salt, and lukewarm water and let sit at room temperature for 5 to 10 minutes until it gets nice and frothy.

2. Add the olive oil and honey to the bloom, mix well, and let sit for another minute.

3. Add 2 2/3 cups flour, mix by hand, and let sit for 3 to 4 more minutes.

4. Transfer the dough to a stand mixer fitted with the dough-hook attachment.

5. Add the remaining 4 cups flour and a total of 1/2 cup of any combination of the optional ingredients. Knead the dough for 5 minutes in the stand mixer.

6. Once the dough has been kneaded, remove it from the stand mixer onto a lightly floured surface and cut it in two equal parts. Roughly shape each into a loaf.

7. Line two 5- x 9-inch loaf pans with parchment paper. Transfer each dough loaf to the prepared pan and loosely cover with plastic wrap. Allow the loaves to proof for 1 hour.

8. When the loaves are almost done proofing, preheat your oven to 350°F.

9. Place the loaf pans on a baking sheet and bake for 50 minutes. Rob says, "Do not open the oven during this time! Yes, that means you!" Test the loaves by inserting a toothpick into the center; if it comes out clean, you're done.

10. When the loaves are done, cool them on a cooling rack until they reach room temperature, then remove them from the pans and enjoy with butter and honey.

LINDA'S WILD BLUEBERRY CRUMBLE

MY MOM TAUGHT ME EVERYTHING I KNOW ABOUT COOKING, even though I hated cooking with her. She kept telling me what to do and how to do it, so the experience was very short-lived. I watched her carefully, though, and waited for my parents to leave the house. Then I cooked for Randi (when she wasn't making butter rice with peas) and Lorne, my sister and brother. Nothing has changed with my mother and me in the kitchen, but we have come to terms with the dynamics and it seems to work. She made this crumble once with a cheesecake filling as well, which I still have dreams about.

DOUGH AND CRUMBLE:

1/2 cup	unsalted butter
1/2 cup	shortening
1 cup	white sugar
1	large egg
3 cups	all-purpose flour
1 tsp	baking powder
1/2 tsp	kosher salt

FILLING:

3 pints	wild blueberries
1 cup	white sugar
4 Tbsp	all-purpose flour
	Zest and juice of 1/2 lemon
	Icing sugar, for dusting

1. Preheat the oven to 350°F. For the dough, in a stand mixer, cream together the butter, shortening, and sugar until pale and fluffy, about 5 minutes. Beat the egg and add it to the mixture, with the mixer running.

2. Sift the flour, baking powder, and salt together, and add to the butter mixture. Stir with a wooden spoon to combine, but don't overwork the dough. Reserve 1/2 cup of this dough for the crumble topping.

3. Press the dough into a 10-inch springform pan. Evenly spread it across the bottom and up the sides to within 1 inch of the top of the pan. Put your crust in the fridge while you get the filling together.

4. For the filling, in a bowl, mix together the blueberries, sugar, flour, lemon zest, and juice. Evenly spread it into your crust.

5. To make the crumble topping, add about 1 Tbsp flour to the remaining dough and crumble it overtop the berries.

6. Bake in the preheated oven for 1 1/4 to 1 1/2 hours. Allow to cool a bit, then dust with icing sugar before serving.

...iches   Berkstore   = Gribbens-   The Business

-liver-

-Flatbread-sky to -Fried Chix

Fries   - Bacon Sauvlaki-   Fried Peanut sectiv

croquettes   - Bacon-

Bacon Sausage-   - Bacon nachos / tost

...Cream   -rice -Bok choi

...k-   -Broth -chili   Griddled Corn Bread

-Shitake-   everywhere

-Brownrice Bowl

For set the wings-   -Fried chix-berk-   Fried Chix con

...l se or se   cocnut

...s Chicken   -vijs-

...va speiria   Fried Chix Tostada

...ickle wings   Fried Smoked Pork Belly

...t pepper wings   -jicama slaw t salad

- chix Fried onions

- Bacon Fried mushrooms

- French Toast Crunch-msf

Fried Salmon skin -smoked-   French Toast Crunch   vac

               lep

Peking Chicken   -onion

Peking Duck

Bunny   Texas

PANTRY RECIPES

DUCK SALT

6	dried bay leaves
1 1/2 Tbsp	chili flakes
4 Tbsp	dried thyme
4 1/2 Tbsp	black peppercorns
2 Tbsp	fennel seeds
3 Tbsp	juniper berries
3 3/4 cups	kosher salt, or 1/2 box

1. Blend all spices in a spice grinder until they're quite fine.

2. Mix spices and salt in a bowl.

3. Store in a mason jar until needed.

BARBECUE SPICE

4 Tbsp	garlic powder
5 Tbsp	onion powder
2 Tbsp	cayenne pepper
3 Tbsp	chili powder
4 Tbsp	mustard powder
5 Tbsp	ground cumin
8 Tbsp	paprika
4 Tbsp	kosher salt
5 Tbsp	white sugar

1. Mix all ingredients together in a bowl.

2. Store in a mason jar until ready to use.

FINGER CHILI HOT SAUCE

1 lb	red finger chilies (you can substitute any other red chili depending on how hot you want this)
10 cloves	garlic
1/2 cup	maple syrup
1 cup	ketchup
1 Tbsp	kosher salt
3 Tbsp	white sugar
2 cups	apple cider vinegar

1. Remove the stems from your chilies, but leave the seeds in.

2. Roughly chop the chilies and garlic.

3. Place all the ingredients in a blender and puree. Let the blender run for a while or the chili skins won't break down.

4. Transfer the sauce to a tightly sealed container and let it sit and ferment at room temperature for 24 hours.

5. Divide the sauce into small jam jars and refrigerate. This should last for a couple of months if stored properly.

CAROLINA BARBECUE SAUCE

1 quart	apple cider vinegar
1 cup	white sugar
1 Tbsp	chili flakes

1. Put all ingredients in a pot and bring up to a simmer for 5 minutes.

2. Pour into a container and cool before using.

CHILI GARLIC JAZZ

2 cups	roughly chopped garlic
1 cup	roughly chopped red finger chilies
1 1/2 cups	canola oil

1. Preheat the oven to 250°F. Put the chopped garlic and chilies in a food processor and buzz them for about 2 to 3 minutes or until they're as broken down as you can get them. Add a bit of canola oil if necessary.

2. Once the garlic and chilies have broken down, pour them into a small oven-safe pot, add the remaining canola oil, and mix well with a spoon. The oil should come just over the top of the veg once it has settled, but this may vary depending on your pot. Add a bit more oil if needed.

3. Cover the pot and put into the preheated oven for 45 to 60 minutes. It should smell nice and toasty and not raw at all when done.

4. Cool and put aside in your fridge. This will last for a couple of months if stored properly in a sealed jar.

BLUE CHEESE DRESSING

4 oz	Ermite blue cheese, or your favorite
1/3 cup	sour cream
1/4 cup	buttermilk
3 Tbsp	apple cider vinegar
2 tsp	dijon mustard
3 Tbsp	mayo
1/3 cup	olive oil

1. Place the cheese, sour cream, buttermilk, vinegar, mustard, and mayo in a blender. Turn on and fully blend the ingredients.

2. While the blender is still running, slowly pour in the olive oil to emulsify.

3. Chill in the fridge before using.

RANCH DRESSING

1 cup	mayo
1 cup	buttermilk
1 cup	sour cream
1/4 tsp	cayenne pepper
1/2 tsp	celery salt
1/4 tsp	onion powder
1/2 bunch	fresh chives, finely chopped
2 sprigs	fresh tarragon, leaves stripped from stems and finely chopped

1. In a bowl, whisk all ingredients together until very smooth.

2. Refrigerate for a couple of hours in a sealed container to let the flavors come out before using.

TARTAR SAUCE

2 Tbsp	small-diced shallots
2 Tbsp	small-diced pickles
2 Tbsp	finely chopped capers
2 Tbsp	chopped fresh parsley
2 Tbsp	chopped fresh chives
2 Tbsp	chopped fresh tarragon
2 Tbsp	chopped fresh dill
1 cup	mayo
2 dashes	Tabasco
	Zest of 1/2 lemon

1. Mix all ingredients together in a bowl.

2. Refrigerate in a sealed container for an hour before serving.

BLUEBERRY JAM

4 cups	frozen wild blueberries
1 cup	white sugar
1/2 tsp	kosher salt
1 1/2 Tbsp	fresh lemon juice

1. Place the blueberries, sugar, and salt in a large pot and gently bring up to a simmer over medium heat.

2. Allow to simmer and reduce a bit; this should take about 15 minutes.

3. Once your jam has reached your preferred consistency, stir in the lemon juice, transfer the jam to small jars, and cool. Store in the fridge for up to 1 month.

SOUR CHERRY JAM

2 lb	frozen sour cherries in juice (no sugar added) (see note)
1 cup	apricot glaze or jam

1. Thaw the cherries and place a colander over a large bowl. Transfer the cherries to the colander and drain all of the juice from them, making sure to reserve the juice. Press gently if necessary to remove all of the juice.

2. Place the cherry juice in a medium pot over medium heat, and reduce the juice by half. Mix in the apricot glaze.

3. Mix the cherries back into the juice and muck it around a bit to make sure that the cherries are all coated in the juice.

4. Cool the jam, then divide it into small jars. Store in the fridge for up to 1 month.

NOTE: If you can't find sour cherries, you can use 1 1/4 lb frozen cherries and 2 cups pure cherry juice.

COCKTAIL SAUCE

1 cup	ketchup
1/2 cup	prepared horseradish, well drained
6 dashes	Tabasco
6 dashes	Worcestershire
1 tsp	kosher salt

1. In a bowl, mix all of the ingredients together and refrigerate in a sealed container for a couple of hours before using.

PICKLED CHILIES

PICKLING LIQUID:

1 cup	white vinegar
1 cup	water
1 cup	white sugar
1 tsp	kosher salt
2 cups	fresh jalapeño rings
2 cups	red finger chili rings

1. Combine all pickling liquid ingredients in a pot and bring up to a boil.

2. Place the jalapeño and red finger chili rings in a large bowl. Pour the hot pickling liquid over the chilies.

3. Allow to cool for 1 to 2 hours before serving.

MONTPELIER BUTTER

1 lb	unsalted butter
	Kosher salt
1/2 bunch	fresh parsley
1/2 bunch	watercress
1/4 cup	mayo
3	salted anchovy fillets
1 Tbsp	chopped capers
1 Tbsp	chopped cornichons
4 Tbsp	finely chopped shallots
1/4 bunch	fresh chives, chopped
1/4 bunch	fresh tarragon, chopped
1/4 bunch	fresh dill, chopped

1. Cube your butter and place it in a stand mixer with the paddle attachment. Whip the butter until it is super-soft and at room temperature.

2. In a pot of salty boiling water, blanch the parsley and watercress together for 30 seconds, then shock in an ice-water bath until completely chilled.

3. Squeeze out all of the liquid from the herbs, give them a rough chop, put them in a blender, and puree.

4. In a large bowl, mix the mayo, anchovies, capers, cornichons, shallots, chives, tarragon, and dill. Fold in the butter.

5. You can roll this in a log to take slices from later or chill in a block and use as needed.

ACKNOWLEDGMENTS

FROM ANTHONY AND CHRIS:

A huge helping of thanks to the brilliant team at Appetite by Random House for supporting this book and working so hard to make this beautiful dream a reality. Kristin Cochrane, Robert McCullough, and Scott Sellers for signing off on this meshuggeneh project. Zoe Maslow, editor nonpareil, without you we'd be lost. Scott Richardson, our designer, for his impeccable aesthetic and immense talent. Lana Okerlund, our copyeditor, your eagle-eyes kept us from embarrassing ourselves. To our respective literary agents: Amy Moore Benson from Meridian Artists for doing all the stuff Anthony never wanted to do and helping him pour his ever-loving, tortured soul on to the white boards, and Sam Hiyate from the Rights Factory for thinking big and never missing a beat.

FROM ANTHONY:

My extremely talented and beautiful photographer, Kayla Rocca. You deserve so much more for putting up with all my bullshit and craziness. Absolutely no other photographer or girlfriend would have put up with me and the way I wanted to do this book. YOU are the only one I ever could have or would have wanted to take this journey with. Thank you for everything and I love you so much.

Thanks to my writing partner, Chris Johns, for coming to my rescue to write this book. You are amazing for seeing the vision and believing in it, and for making the impossible dream come true. Thank you, CJ.

My best friend and business partner, Robert Wilder, for forever having confidence in me and everything we do. Feels so good when someone has your back the way you have mine. I love you and your family, Jackie, Ethan, and Roan, for being the support we both need and all the love to fit.

To be clear, I never wanted to write a cookbook. Zoe Maslow, my editor and friend, said I could do it any way I wanted to. Thank you for that, Zozo, and for being so strong and listening to all of my crazy ideas. To be clear, I do not want to write another cookbook, but after seeing what you did . . . okay, let's do it again. You are the best.

My sweet son, Simon Thorne Rose, for the constant moral support and for listening to hip hop on the way to school and educating me on the new sound of the kids these days.

My folks, Linda and Joel, for putting up with my childhood angst and giving me this deep love of food and wine. My brothers and sisters, Randi, Lorne, Craig, and Lindsi, for never criticizing anything they eat at my restaurants.

My nieces and nephews, Eli, Noa, Lila, Charlie, Riley, and Sid. For always telling the truth and wanting cauliflower soup forever and ever.

Desiree Sabato, never my personal assistant but always protecting me. Thanks
for loving Swiss Chalet as much as I do. All the restaurants owe you so much
for making us sweeter people. Many more years to go.

Kevin Gilmour, my culinary director and longtime friend. This book would not
be here without you. Thanks so much for making it a possibility and for calling me when you didn't really want that other job and for realizing that when
I said I would make a job to fit your needs, I meant it.

Jennifer Bubleit, my DOO, for making it all run smoothly, so I can do whatever
it is I want to do whenever I want to do it.

Debbie Rothstein, for keeping us afloat, writing all the cheques, and giving
away all our monies. Pennies on the dollar.

The Team at Rose and Sons and Big Crow: Dawn, Sean, Spencer, and Erik for
making my favorite restaurant sing.

The Team at Fat Pasha: Lauren, Jeremy, and Mike for making the Good Jew Food
the big thing it should be. Jerry as Moses.

The Team at Schmaltz: Josh, Sean, and Mo for schmearing and slicing and making
the word "appetizing" mean something again.

The Team at Bar Begonia and Madame Boeuf: Marla, Lauren, Jesse, and Mike for
making all things great from burgers to cassoulet and martinis to slushies.

All our suppliers and purveyors and builders. All the cooks and servers. We
would be nothing without you.

Our silent investors and supporters, Kevin, Steven, Randy, Michelle, Kathleen,
and Sandy. Thank you for your vision.

Bonnie Stern, forever supporting me and everything I do.

Jonathon Waxman, for the elegant simplicity and his beautiful face.

FROM CHRIS:

Thanks to my co-author, Anthony Rose, for being such a mensch. You made
writing this book a sheer pleasure.

To my beautiful wife, Jillian, for her endless enthusiasm, brilliance, and
love of adventure.

Harper, you're only three years old, but you make my life better in every
worthwhile way possible.

And to the rest of my family: Suzanne, Dave, Carolyn, Leslie, Tyler, Leon,
Larry, Heather, Brian, Lola.